Kim Oates AM, MD, DSc, MHP, FRACP, FRCP, FAFPHM, FRACMA, DCH is a paediatrician who trained in Sydney, London and Boston. Most of his professional life has been at the Royal Alexandra Hospital for Children, initially when it was the Children's Hospital at Camperdown and now The Children's Hospital at Westmead. Various roles there have included Head of the hospital's Child Development and Child Protection Units and Chair of the Division of Medicine.

Kim then spent 12 years as Professor of Paediatrics and Child Health at the University of Sydney, based at The Children's Hospital, before becoming the hospital's Chief Executive, a position he held for eight years until 2006. He is currently Emeritus Professor of Paediatrics at the University of Sydney, where he is involved in reviewing the postgraduate medical curriculum.

The author or editor of 13 books, he has a long-standing interest in child development, child behaviour, the problems of child abuse and neglect, as well as advocacy on behalf of children. He has received a range of national and international awards for his work, including the Nathalie Masse International Prize for Research in the Field of Childhood from the International Children's Centre in Paris and the Kempe Award from the USA for 'Outstanding contributions to the community on behalf of children', the first time this has been awarded outside that country.

Kim and Robyn have been married for 40 years, have three children and eight grandchildren and are both well aware that they still have lots to learn.

so now you're a
GRANDPARENT

Dr Kim Oates

illustrations by Nik Scott

SIMON & SCHUSTER
AUSTRALIA

PREFACE

I have to admit it. I'm a grandparent. And so is my wife. We love it. So now you're immediately suspicious. You wonder if this book is just therapy for an elderly chap to say how wonderful his grandchildren are and how idyllic grandparenting is. Believe me, there are books like this (mostly in the northern hemisphere); I've read them, and the saccharine flavour definitely leaves an aftertaste.

So why did I write it? There are several reasons. One is that when I looked at what was on offer in large bookshops, I found many books on child-rearing and parenting, but almost nothing on grandparenting. How strange! Children generally have two parents, but they have four grandparents, or more or less, depending on remarriage or death. It seemed to me, with such a dearth of information, that this important relationship has been overlooked.

The other reason is that I am a paediatrician, so I'm supposed to know a lot about kids. I have certainly seen a lot and talked with a lot of parents and grandparents. Often they are anxious, trying to do a good job (and they usually are) and looking for reassurance. So this book is a way of passing on some of that experience; what I've learned from parents and grandparents and providing a little reassurance.

Many of the smart ideas in this book come from my wife Robyn, either as I wrote it and discussed it with her or as I absorbed her ideas over the last 40 years (we're not really old, we just married young!).

What I hope this book won't do is embarrass our children or our grandchildren. There are lots of cute stories I could tell about them, but they may not like it and you would probably think that the stories you have about your own children or grandchildren are cuter anyway.

KIM OATES
Sydney 2007

ACKNOWLEDGMENTS

There are lots of people who have helped and taught me over the years. My colleagues at The Children's Hospital at Westmead, the children and their parents whom I've helped look after and who taught me so much; my international colleagues including Dr Berry Brazelton from Boston Children's Hospital; and of course my wife, Robyn and our family, who taught me the most and our grandchildren, from whom I'm still learning.

I'm also grateful to my own parents for a wonderful childhood, for teaching me about tolerance and caring and who, presumably due to some strange quirk related to the toilet training technique used in those distant days, left me with a scatological sense of humour, which still surfaces at times.

Special thanks to Glenda Downing and her editorial team at Simon & Schuster who have provided wise advice and encouragement and who gently reined me in at those times when I became over-enthusiastic.

A number of organisations, websites and authors have been helpful including some of the writings of Gay Ochiltree, Jennifer Hetherington, Jan Backhouse, Joy Goodfellow, Judy Laverty, Kerry Carrington and Margot Fitzpatrick. Kidsafe Australia, The Australian Institute of Family Studies, The Australian Institute of Health and Welfare, The Australian Bureau of Statistics, The American Psychological Association, the Australian Parliamentary Library, the Raising Children Network, Compassionate Friends and the BBC UK website have been valuable resources.

Some of the illustrations about children and families are composites of several situations I've seen professionally, while other individual cases have had their identities and any identifying details substantially altered. Any omissions or errors are of my own making.

1

Are You Ready?

One day your child will visit or the telephone will ring and you learn that you are to be a grandparent. You say something like: 'That's wonderful darling. I'm so pleased', but inside you may have a variety of reactions which may include:

'It's absolutely wonderful, I'm so happy.'

'It's about time. I was beginning to think it would never happen.'

'Me! A grandparent. I'm much too young.'

'That's lovely, but what will happen to her career and what will they expect of me?'

'That means I'm going to be sleeping with a grandfather' (or sleeping with a grandmother, depending on who you are).

Or a mixture of all of these feelings, plus others I haven't thought of.

Remember when you decided to have your own children? Most of us were able to plan when we would have them. But when you become a grandparent you aren't involved in the plan at all. You just get told.

Having said all that, in a world where so many new things are talked about in superlatives and later are found to be over-rated, grandparenting is the only thing that is *not* over-rated. Once you've sorted out your own feelings and realised that your children's focus will now change, and after you've resolved some of the practical issues, you'll be pretty impressed with the change that has occurred in your life.

BEING A GRANDPARENT

Some of you might recall grandparents who mostly sat around, had a rather musty smell, lots of wrinkles, talked a lot about the past and seemed out of touch with the present. You don't have to be like that, unless you want to. Being a grandparent can keep you young. It can stop you from ageing quite as quickly as you would otherwise and it gives you an excuse to do dumb things. I know one grandfather whose six-year-old grand-daughter invited him to her themed Wizard of Oz birthday party on the condition that he dressed up as the Scarecrow, joined in the games and entertained the other six year olds by singing *If I Only Had a Brain*.

But first you may wonder if you really want all of these changes, or even if you are ready for them. These are some of the questions which may arise:

Am I too young?

Will grandparenting complicate my life? This is particularly relevant if you have recently retired and are planning lots of trips and leisure in retirement.

How much time will I have to give up?

If they ask me to do lots of child care, will I have to give up my own job?

How much time should I spend with my grandchildren?

Enjoy your grandchildren, but don't put your life on hold for them. Keep living a full life. Enjoy the things you do now: your marital relationship, your friends, your hobbies, and other interests. Make room for your grandchildren in your life, but you don't have to neglect all the other relationships and activities you enjoy.

You'll eventually sort these things out. We'll look at some of them later. In the meantime, it's reassuring that the great thing about being a grandparent is that you don't have to act like a parent when the grandchildren are around. We obviously have to be sensible and safe, but we aren't responsible for all of the details of their lives, in contrast to when we were parents of young children.

This is a relief (who'd want all that again?) and a wonderful opportunity. With our grandchildren we have time to watch and learn and wonder. We usually didn't have that sort of time with our own children. We were too busy doing things for them. We noticed that they developed but we didn't have the luxury of the time to watch them develop. Being a grandparent is a unique opportunity to enjoy your offspring. And you can usually tailor the dose so that it is just right.

What will they call you?

This is pretty important as the name will stick. Grandpa and Grandma are the more traditional names. They may carry memories of elderly, unexciting, inactive folk, certainly not the correct description for you, at least for the present. You may be perfectly happy with one of the more traditional names such as:

Grandma	Nanna
Grandpa	Grandmother
Pop	Grandfather
Papa	Granddad
Nan	Gramps
Nana	

But if you're not, you'll need to be creative. Whatever you decide, keep in mind that it:

- may be for the long haul. Because we are living longer, some of us will be grandparents for more than 50 per cent of our lives
- shouldn't embarrass you or your grandchildren as time passes. 'Mumu' or 'Grumbles' may be cute for a two year old to use but may not have quite the same cachet when your 16-year-old grandson calls it out to you from across the street
- should be something that can easily be pronounced by the child. If 'Grandpa' comes out as 'Grumpy', you may be labelled with that for the rest of your life, especially if it matches your character

- needs to be different from the name chosen by the other set of grandparents. Yes, remember, there is another set of grandparents. (More about them in the next chapter.)

You can just use your own christian name or you can precede it by a grandparent-type name such as 'Grandpa George' or 'Grandma Judy', providing, of course, that your name actually is George or Judy. This may also help distinguish you from the other set of grandparents.

THE NEW GRANDCHILD

Everyone coos and goos when they see a new baby. They say things like, 'Isn't she lovely' and, 'Don't you think she looks a little bit like Aunt Agatha', 'Yes, but I think she has Uncle Bertram's nose'. Frankly, I don't know how people can make these deductions on day one of life. Some newborns are particularly cute, but others are wrinkled and blotchy, perhaps with an odd-shaped head, the result of being pushed through a birth canal whose boundaries are a bone-hard pelvis.

Somehow or other, we fall in love with our children whatever they look like, but it's not always immediate and for fathers it might take a little longer until the tiny creature completely captivates you as you fall under her spell. It's similar for grandparents, too. So if it takes you a little while to fall in love, don't worry. It's highly likely that you'll be totally besotted before long.

You may have to dredge your memory to remember what it was like having a baby. You might be surprised to find that things have changed:

- Many babies are now born in more user-friendly birthing centres attached to hospitals and go home within four to 24 hours. Some may be born at home. Of course, in our day babies were born at home, too, or were born in a taxi, but that was just because they were in a hurry to arrive in the world.

- There are about three times as many immunisation shots as when we had our children. These days the immunisation schedule is more complex and is regularly revised as new immunisations become available. Immunisations that have become available since you had your children include mumps, chickenpox, meningococcal disease and hepatitis B, as well as Haemophilus influenzae (Hib) immunisation, which prevents some forms of pneumonia and meningitis. For up-to-date details see www.immunise.health.gov.au or call Immunise Australia on 1800 671 811.
- Safety standards are a lot higher. There are all sorts of safety standards that have to be met for infant furniture and equipment and it's a good idea to check for these when you're buying anything for the new arrival.
- The range of products available for babies today is mind-boggling. There are strollers designed to look like sports buggies, double and tandem strollers, folding high chairs (choose one that meets Australian safety standards so that it won't fold up when in use), portable high chairs, baby seats that hook onto the family meal table, even leatherette high chairs (don't ask me why), baby carriers which are sophisticated backpacks, and baby holders and restraints which rock, swing, bounce and play music.
- With the rise in both parents working, there is a variety of day care, including long day care allowing many mothers to return to work much sooner than a generation ago.
- fathers are often more involved in child-rearing and child care. Many modern fathers can organise their lives so that they can have a greater share in child-raising. It's no longer regarded as 'women's work' for men to cuddle their young children, help prepare meals, feed them, bathe them and change dirty nappies.
- Families aren't quite what they used to be. There have been many changes in society since you were a young parent. The taboos against marrying into a different racial or religious group are largely gone. Not all parents living together with

children have got around to getting married. Some homosexual couples have children. Many more mothers also hold down jobs and child care is much more widely available.

So although the basics of child-rearing are much the same, a great deal has changed. You'll still be able to pass on your advice and wisdom, but you'll also learn plenty and you'll be quite impressed and rather proud as you watch your children do the parenting.

Your children may ask for advice and you'll hope they do, but one thing that you've already given them is a good dose of your own genetic material. Each of your children receives 50 per cent of their genes from you and 50 per cent from your partner. They give 50 per cent of their genes (that's 25 per cent of yours) and 50 per cent of their partner's genes to each of their children. So when you see some of your more desirable characteristics appearing in your grandchildren, you may want to quietly take some of the credit. If you see some of your less desirable characteristics on display, they may be from your genetic influence, too, although you'll probably be tempted to feel it's most likely to have come from 'the other side of the family'.

One recent piece of Australian research has even suggested that the diet of pregnant mothers can influence the activity of some genes, not only in their own children but in their grandchildren as well. How could this be? The researchers found that a nutritious diet in pregnancy can 'switch off' the gene responsible for obesity and diabetes. They were surprised to find that this effect was carried into the grandchildren, who were also likely to switch off the activity of these genes if their grandmothers had been taking a nutritious, vitamin-enriched diet when they were pregnant.

Before you become too excited, you need to know that this research was done in mice and the diabetes gene in mice is not exactly the same as ours. However, it does provide further evidence about how the activity of genes can be influenced by the environment.

THE NEW GRANDPARENT

The baby boomers are becoming grandparents. The stereotype of the wizened, authoritarian, not particularly active, sometimes crotchety, sometimes twinkle-eyed, but always old, grandparent has changed. Grandparents now live longer, are usually better educated and are healthier than the grandparents we had. They are active, and many live into their eighties and beyond, often maintaining much of their physical and mental ability. As pointed out earlier, this increase in life expectancy means that some people will be grandparents for more than half their lives. So if you've just become a grandparent, it's a life sentence, although not a bad one. You'd better get used to it.

Of course there are some people in our age range who wonder if they ever will become grandparents, as many couples now delay having children until their thirties. Even so, when the grandchildren eventually do arrive you can still look forward to 20 or 30 years of grandparenting.

Few of us had grandmothers who had a paid job. In the 1940s women were often expected to leave work when they married. Now

...the stereotype has changed

many grandmothers are in full-time or part-time paid employment. This raises the issue of how much time they will have available to devote to a grandparenting role. Some modern grandmothers have the conflict of needing to participate in paid employment and also being asked to (and often wanting to) provide care for their grandchildren so that their daughter or daughter-in-law can work. Some of these modern grandparents even have a triple whammy: maintaining their own employment, assisting with the care of their grandchildren and being involved in caring for their own elderly parents who may be in their eighties and nineties. No wonder they feel tired.

In the past, grandparents were often the family experts in child-rearing, living with the family and playing a role in child-rearing as well as passing on the accumulated wisdom of previous generations.

Now there are nuclear families, blended families, step-families, single-parent families and same-sex families. Experts in child-rearing abound. There are magazine articles, TV shows, books (like this one) and even how-to-do-it courses which all compete for the role grandparents used to have in the past.

Modern grandparents use the internet, email their grandchildren and send text messages. Well, some do. Others still have difficulty programming the DVD player.

Because grandparents will be in their role for so long, the role will change over time as more grandchildren are born, grandchildren grow up and have children of their own, family members may separate, remarry and suffer from a variety of health problems including mental illness, while eventually the grandparents become old and frail. Depressing, isn't it? So make the most of it while you can and grow old in the job gracefully. Or disgracefully, if that's your preference.

WHAT SORT OF GRANDPARENT DO YOU WANT TO BE?

The type of grandparent you want to be will depend on what sort of person you are right now. It's unlikely that you will have a personality transplant on becoming a grandparent, although one of the advantages of ageing is that we do tend to mellow, become a little wiser, and some of the rough edges of our earlier days start to smooth over. It's a great opportunity to be a role model, someone your grandchildren can respect and learn from. Whatever you want to be like, your grandchildren's impression of you may be different and a little more basic. I asked a group of three to four year olds to tell me about their grandparents:

Jessica, three-and-a-half: 'One of my grandparents is old'.

Luke, four years: 'My grandpa likes to eat hamburgers and sausages'.

Alicia, four years: 'My grandma drives her car fast when she goes to the gym'.

Jordan, three-and-a-half: 'My grandpa tells me funny jokes. He is a funny clown. He makes me laugh'.

Petra, three years old: 'I love my grandma. She makes me laugh'.

Jack, three-and-a-half: 'My grandma doesn't live with my grandpa'.

Helen, aged four: 'My grandpa is dead'.

Nicholas, four-and-a-half: 'My grandma comes to my house a lot. She is going to come to my school next year'.

Deciding what sort of grandparent you want to be will be determined partly by your underlying personality and other skills. Being a grandparent involves more than just loving your grandchildren. As you become part of their lives, you become an influence in their lives. Some of your roles may include:

- a person like your own grandparents (this will depend on whether you have good memories of them)
- a bringer of gifts
- a childminder
- a keeper of the family history and family traditions
- a storyteller
- a confidante
- an example of a strong religious faith
- someone who teaches kindness, consideration and generosity to all
- reliable and always available

- rather remote or distant
- critical
- grumpy and complaining
- funny
- the family patriarch or matriarch.

The above aren't mutually exclusive. Some types you definitely wouldn't want to emulate. You can probably think of others. It's worth checking your style occasionally to make sure you aren't inadvertently slipping into one of the less charming types of grandparents.

One trap to avoid is trying to satisfy your own needs through your grandchildren. It may seem an opportunity to make up for some of the failings we've all had from time to time as parents, but it's not the grandparents' role to be parents again.

We might also think that our passion for things like music, the theatre, rugby, line dancing, croquet, philately or macramé should be shared and enjoyed by our grandchildren. It probably won't be. After all, they're kids and to them we're pretty old. We can expose them to our interests, if their parents agree. Polite grandchildren may even tolerate them. Occasionally our interest may open up a wonderful world for them, such as music or theatre, but we shouldn't expect them to embrace all the things we like, particularly macramé.

A WORD TO GRANDFATHERS

Can you change a dirty nappy? No, not a wet nappy, I mean a dirty one. Not just a firm, compact one. A runny one. One that leaks out. A real stinker. Did you have much experience of that when you were a young dad or did you leave that special privilege for the young mum?

Child-rearing isn't strictly women's work these days, as you may have noticed. Your son or son-in-law is likely to be much more involved in all aspects of child care than you ever were. One of the few things you and he will have in common is that neither of you did the breastfeeding. However, he's likely to be quite confident, and comfortable about all the rest.

Don't worry. He and his partner won't expect you to be good at all of these things. They understand. But your grandchild may not. Imagine this scenario. You're visiting your 22-month-old grandson. He thinks you're wonderful. He's not quite ready to be toilet trained and after dinner he fills his nappy with something which becomes obvious to all as the smell pervades the room. Mum says, 'Okay Brad, let's change that nappy.' Brad says, in a voice which has a surprising air of authority, 'I want Grandpa to do it!'

What do you do? Do you hide? Do you fake an epileptic fit as a diversionary tactic? Do you flick a quick pass to Nana, saying she is the expert? Do you manfully have a go only to be defeated when Brad starts to wriggle at the crucial moment? These can be testing times for grandfathers who may need to learn skills they had little use for in the past.

In many ways it's easier for the new grandmother than the new grandfather. Grandmothers relate well to babies because of their past experience and have lots of useful advice they are able to pass on. They can help in practical ways. Grandfathers may feel irrelevant and of less use. Many men and grandfathers don't relate all that well to babies initially and it may take a little longer to fall in love and become totally captivated.

Some grandfathers may not be as good at communicating with toddlers, compared with their wives and because of work commitments they may have fewer opportunities to develop these skills. It's certainly worth working on them and taking every opportunity to be with the grandchildren. They will teach you communication skills. They'll want to involve you in their games and when it comes to a rough-and-tumble physical activity, this is where you may excel.

Grandfathers have wisdom to pass on to their grandchildren. They are often the best ones at playing imaginative games and telling stories. Remember, you don't have to make up the imaginative game. Just be available to let your grandchild involve you in it. It may not be your idea of a Sunday afternoon to crawl under the outdoor table with your grandchild to escape from a marauding lion, but it can be great fun. You've got nothing to lose but your dignity.

IT WILL CHANGE YOUR LIFE

Remember when you had total control over your children? As they grew older, went to school, made friends and grew more independent your influence became less.

Some parents let go too soon, not giving enough guidance to their children and exerting too little control. Other parents never seem to let go. They don't encourage independence and may even remain controlling and enmeshed in their children's lives after they have left home. Being a good parent is about being able to let go at the right rate. By the time your children are parents (and hopefully well before this) you should have totally let go. Control should be long gone, now your role is to be helpful and supportive.

Your children's relationships with you will change, too. They now have a baby, a totally new focus and their lives are changed. They have different priorities. They don't have the time they previously had for you, although they may now want you to do more things for them. You may even feel a trifle jealous.

You may be a reluctant grandparent, initially at least. You may be the sort of adult who doesn't get on all that well with babies and toddlers but relates better to older children.

You may have a very busy life. Time may be scarce and you may worry that their expectations of you as a grandparent may exceed your own view of the type of grandparent you want to be. You may not have any of these feelings. Or you may have some of them initially, only for them to fade away as you fall in love with your grandchild and swell with pride as you watch your children display parenting skills you never knew they had.

As we learn most about being a parent in the early years of our lives, based on the way our parents cared for us, you can take part of the credit for some of the good things you see in the new parents.

It can also be tiring looking after grandchildren. Your children may assume that you have as much energy as they have. Staying fit, or becoming fit, is an important part of grandparenting.

It's smart to think of and decide a few things in advance. Some of these you will want to talk about as a couple, while others you may want to discuss and agree with your children, such as the following subjects.

Child care

What will be the expectations about child care? You'll certainly want to help out at times. Do you want a regular commitment? Will you have to give up your own employment to provide child care for your grandchildren? How much leisure time are you prepared to give up? It's best to have clear communication about these things early on so that expectations on both sides are realistic. It's okay to be flexible as circumstances change, but it's also important to honour any commitment you make as a grandparent.

Other grandchildren are likely to follow, perhaps in this family or from your other children. In terms of fairness, it's good to make commitments equally to all your grandchildren, so it's perhaps not all that wise to make a major commitment to the very first one, particularly if that level is something you can't provide for all the subsequent grandchildren.

Financial assistance

You may be in a position to help financially and, if so, do it. But remember that a commitment to do something for one grandchild, just as for child care, may also turn out to be a commitment for subsequent grandchildren.

It's not all that clever, in a fit of generosity at the christening speech, to assure your child that because your grandchild is so wonderful, you are going to pay all the fees and associated expenses so that she can attend your favourite private school. Apart from the fact that she may not want to, she may be the first of 16 grandchildren, a real possibility if there are multiple births within the family. Paying all of those private school fees will be quite a challenge.

Never make a promise you can't keep. It's a good rule for parents and a good rule for grandparents, too. And an important example for your grandchildren.

2

Getting Along with the Parents

It doesn't seem that long ago since you were told you are going to be a grandparent. And now you are. You want to be as helpful as possible. Does one of you move in to help the new parents when they bring the baby home? Do both of you move in? Do you turn up with your bag packed ready to help, only to find that the other set of grandparents has already moved in?

These are some of the things you will want to discuss before the baby is born. It will, of course, depend on your circumstances. It will also depend on how you get along with the new parents. If you are employed, you may need to take leave to help out. On the other hand, your children may be so well organised and independent that they don't need very much help.

It's worth remembering that when a relative does move in to help, it is usually the new mother's own mother. The new grandfather usually stays at home, at least initially. Mothers and daughters often have a special relationship and as long as there is no personality clash, it's a good time to help out. If you are the grandparents on the new father's side, you may feel a little left out, but your turn will come.

If you do move in, what will you do and how long will you stay? It's wise to have realistic expectations for your role. This means realistic expectations for yourself and also realistic expectations on the part of the new parents. You don't move in to spend lots of time cuddling the new baby while mum does the household chores and looks after the other children.

The best way to help is to roll up your sleeves, do a lot of the domestic work and free up mum and dad to get to know their new baby. Your role might include looking after the other children, (who are also your grandchildren), taking them to school, cutting lunches and performing various taxi duties. You can shop, clean, field phone calls, cook, wash and be generally useful. Just avoid the temptation to shop for things they won't eat, clean up things which don't need cleaning and reorganise the house so much that they can't find anything after you've left.

It's not all domestic drudgery. You'll be able to be supportive, give advice and, if you have any energy left, get to know your new grandchild.

It's not unusual for new mothers to feel a bit flat a few days after the thrill and excitement of giving birth. Most mums get over the 'post-baby blues' fairly quickly and a supportive, considerate partner and good family support certainly help. In some cases though, there is a real problem and postnatal depression sets in. This is much more common than most people think. Just over 10 per cent of mothers suffer from postnatal depression. This can interfere with their ability to tune into their baby's needs. The sad thing is that postnatal depression is often overlooked, with only about 50 per cent of cases being correctly diagnosed. It's important that it's not missed as good professional psychological support can speed up the lifting of the depression. It can also help the husband to be more sensitive to the mother's needs as well as to the baby's needs.

It's not the job of parents or in-laws to diagnose postnatal depression, unless that's your area of professional expertise. But it is helpful to know that it's not uncommon and that if it is diagnosed in your family, it's nothing to be ashamed of or embarrassed about and that the sensitive support of grandparents can help.

The arrival of a new grandchild may bring up a few areas of disagreement. What if your child's partner (and therefore one set of the grandparents) comes from a different ethnic background with different expectations about a whole range of child-rearing techniques and traditions? The solution may not be easy, although some of these potential areas of conflict can be headed off at the pass by a thoughtful discussion between the parents and grandparents before the child is born. In the end, it will be the child's mum and dad who make the decision and once they do, it's your job to support them in it, even though it may be tempting to rehash your views every now and then. That's one of those temptations that need to be firmly resisted.

One of the very early decisions your daughter or daughter-in-law will make is about breastfeeding, whether to or not and, if so, for how long. There is plenty of good medical evidence for the benefits of breastfeeding, particularly the advantages to the baby's immune system in reducing the chance of infections, such as gastroenteritis. However, it's a personal decision. If you are consulted about this decision the main thing is to be supportive and not to make her feel guilty if she chooses not to breastfeed or if she only does so for a short time.

One piece of recent research may be useful to know. It will also make you look like someone who is up to date with the latest medical research which may enhance your reputation as a wise parent or perhaps diminish it as a know-all, depending on how you convey the information.

In the 1980s and 1990s some studies suggested that children who were breastfed as babies had a higher IQ. The difference was about four IQ points. Not much really, but if your grandchild is hoping to get into a highly competitive university course, based on end of school results, it might make that little bit of difference.

The information from these studies naturally caused some anxiety to parents and a little guilt in some mothers. In 2006, a large study, which followed over 5000 children from birth, found that breastfeeding had little or no effect on intelligence. The difference of about four IQ points noted in the studies from the 1980s and 1990s was found to be related almost entirely to the mother's own IQ, rather than to whether or not the baby was breastfed.

The researchers confirmed these findings in a really neat additional study. They compared children in families where one child was breastfed and the other wasn't and found no difference in the children's intelligence. The conclusion: while breastfeeding has many advantages for the child and mother, raising the child's intelligence is unlikely to be one of them.

Sometimes the birth of a child gets parents thinking about getting married at some stage, even though they may have been living together happily for several years. This development, along with other milestones, like the possible christening of the new baby, could cause some friction in the family.

What do you do if the two sets of grandparents have different views about religion? One pair wants their grandchild christened into a particular religious faith while the other pair may be antagonistic towards anything vaguely religious and may prefer a simple naming ceremony. Situations like this can sometimes be resolved by having two different ceremonies, the appropriate religious ceremony and perhaps a later naming ceremony where all of the members of the wider family can participate.

I remember Paul and Vicki, who found an ideal solution for this situation. They had been together for six years and already had a three-year-old boy, Andy, but when their next child was on the way they thought it would be nice to get the family together for a wedding. There was a variety of religious views in the extended family so that they decided to opt for a spring-time civil ceremony in a lovely garden and, building on the reputation they already had for efficiency, combined the wedding ceremony with a naming ceremony for Andy. Members of the family who had rarely spoken to each other did so and even formidable Aunt Ellen, who had assumed the position of custodian of family etiquette, agreed that it had been a great day.

REMEMBER WHO'S THE BOSS

This is not a subject for debate. The people who make the rules and the decisions about your grandchild's life are the parents; not the grandparents. You may find that you need to bite your tongue at times. It's okay to give advice quietly and sensitively, but you'll have to stick to the parents' rules. Even though you're 'older and wiser' (well, 'older' anyway), it's not at all wise to contradict your children in front of your grandchildren. Show respect for your children's decisions. Support them, don't undermine them. The golden rule is that your grandchildren's parents have the last word as far as their children are concerned.

THINGS ARE DIFFERENT NOW

When we were parents we were told to do things in a certain way. To do otherwise, we were told, would be at the baby's peril. A generation later, many of the rules seem to have changed. They clearly weren't as important as we were told.

The remarkable thing about babies is that they are both vulnerable and resilient. They need to be fed, kept warm, protected and stimulated because of their small size, vulnerability and developing brain. But they also generally turn out well whether breastfed or bottle fed, burped or not burped and swaddled or not swaddled. So we shouldn't live in the past and base our advice entirely on what we were told. Here is a quick rundown on some of the things you will encounter.

Sleep position

One of the biggest changes since we had our children is that babies are now put to sleep on their backs. We were told not to do this in case they burped up some milk, which then went down the wrong way. It has now been quite clearly shown by pioneering New Zealand and Australian research that the incidence of Sudden Infant Death Syndrome (SIDS) is halved as a result of changing the sleeping position. SIDS is the most common cause of death between one month and one year of age. We still don't know for sure what causes SIDS but there is now no doubt that putting babies to sleep on their backs has saved many hundreds, probably thousands, of lives. The best way to remember the correct sleep position is: 'back to sleep'.

Bottles and milk

Milk is no longer boiled. The old process of boiling milk was good for killing germs but also sometimes caused problems if too much of the water content of the milk was boiled away, leaving milk which was too concentrated for the baby's immature body to cope with. Milk also no longer needs to be warmed. Many babies are happy to drink it straight from the refrigerator.

Bottles are also no longer sterilised by boiling. The American Academy of Pediatrics says that sterilisation of bottles and boiling of water is no longer necessary as long as your water comes from a municipal water supply (as opposed to rainwater coming from your roof into a tank) and if you use a dishwasher. However, many parents like to boil water and allow it to cool before mixing it with milk powder and also like to use sterilising solutions for bottles and teats.

Food

An abundance of commercial baby foods is available. Your family might decide that baby food from cans and jars is not for their baby and may prepare all their food at home. This is fine, but if they decide to go with the commercial baby food, don't despair. It's made to rigorous dietetic standards and as long as the baby receives a balanced range—that is, cereals, vegetables and meat—rather than too many desserts, he'll get all the nutritional value he needs.

Wait a minute, you just dipped your finger into the jar of brains and vegies and it tastes disgusting. How can this be good for baby? You think it tastes disgusting because it is very low in salt. A low salt intake is good for the baby's future and present health, but as you've grown used to a salty taste, its absence makes you think there is something wrong with the food.

Bibs

Babies still use bibs, sometimes. But now they do up behind the neck with Velcro. What an advance. No more frustration as you struggle to untangle the knots in those thin, bib tapes.

Nappies

Most parents these days use disposable nappies. If cloth nappies are used, they are held in place by a neat little plastic gadget which, unlike those barbarous nappy pins of our generation, doesn't poke a hole in your finger or worse, in some important part of junior's anatomy, as you apply it.

Time and pressure

There seems to be less time now than in the past. There is also more pressure. Why, no-one knows, but new parents seem to have less time, more activities and more pressure than their own parents had.

There also seems to be more pressure to be an excellent parent, if not a perfect one. Perhaps it's because of all the childcare experts on radio and television and the childcare books which fill shelves in bookstores.

You may be able to reassure your children that people don't have to be perfect parents, just 'good enough parents'. Babies, infants and children need love, consistency, nurturing and positive stimulation. They don't need 24-hour one-on-one stimulation, expensive educational toys or baby education classes. They just like to spend time with people who love them, comfort them, play with them and talk to them: people who are consistent in their care and unconditional in their love. Those tasks aren't all that difficult. They don't cost a lot of money and grandparents can become part of the team that helps to provide them.

...childcare experts

Ideas about methods of discipline have changed, too. There was a time when parents were thought to be derelict in their duties if they did not spank their children. My personal view is that it is wrong to hit children. Many parents now do a great job of raising and disciplining their children without resorting to hitting them. If you are a grandparent who was regularly hit as a child and who smacked your own children, it may be difficult to get used to this concept. See more about methods of discipline in Chapter 3.

BEING SUPPORTIVE

Despite outward confidence, deep down we all feel a little insecure at times. Perhaps some of us feel insecure most of the time! We may feel a little insecure about whether we'll be good grandparents. Well, as you may remember, this is nothing to the insecurity that many new parents feel.

One of the most important things grandparents can do is to support their children in parenting. It's easy to be critical at times and perhaps to voice our criticisms, which isn't a very clever thing to do. The problem is that we tend not to notice when things are going well and usually don't make comments then. When your children are doing a good job, don't just take it for granted. Tell them. Tell them how impressed you are with some aspect of their parenting. And don't do it just once, do it often, but not so often that it becomes meaningless.

I had the good fortune to do some of my paediatric training in Boston with Dr Berry Brazelton. Berry Brazelton is revered in the United States as a wise, sensible paediatrician and an expert in child development. He taught me lots, but one of the most useful things he taught me was to tell parents when they were doing a good job. Even when things aren't going particularly well, you can generally find something positive to say. Paediatricians are usually telling parents what they should do, but when Berry Brazelton praised something a parent had done, you could almost see the parent grow taller. And, of course, they would then be much more ready to accept his advice about what they needed to do to help their child.

Thank you, Berry. It was a valuable lesson that works. So don't forget to tell your children when they are doing a good job.

New parents often need advice. They also often need a lot of support. They may even be a little defensive, keen to show you that they can do a good job and quite sensitive to any hint of criticism. They need reassurance rather than criticism. Sentences that start off with, 'I knew that would happen…' or, 'No wonder…' or, 'I've told you before…' and which then go on to point out the parental defect aren't very helpful.

It's much better to tell your children about some of your failings and discoveries as a parent, such as, 'When you were a baby, I found it helped to…' or, 'What you really liked when you were a baby was to…' You can also build on what they have done and use that opening to give advice.

If you listen to a really good media performer you will notice that they don't avoid the question, as politicians sometimes tend to do. Instead, they answer the question and then add the piece of information they want to get over; for example, 'Yes Amanda, my organisation certainly wants to do that, but the other, equally important thing we want to do is…' People who coach others to develop good media skills call this 'value adding'. You can value add too. It's a good way to give advice in the kitchen and in the living room as well as on the media: 'That's a nice idea and it means you could probably also…'

Despite your most subtle, supportive and reassuring ways of giving advice, it may not always be taken. Just remember how you felt when your parents gave you advice that you didn't need or didn't want. Don't bristle. Don't harp. Just move on and if you turn out to be proven right, remember never resort to saying, 'I told you so', however much you may be tempted.

You may not always agree with your children. The hardest part of being a grandparent is when you don't agree with the way your children are raising your grandchildren. For some grandparents it may be quite a balancing act: supporting the parents, respecting their views and at the same time trying to give guidance in a helpful way. Just remember who is the boss and that if you want lots of access to your grandchildren, you'll need to respect the wishes of their parents.

BABYSITTING

You are asked to come over and mind the children. Or they may be dropped over at your place. Here are some useful tips.

Their house: their rules

You've only come over to babysit, not to change the social order. Respect the parents' rules and views on food, bedtime, snacks and television.

Don't overdo the sweets and treats. You may be asked to pay for the dental bills.

Your house: your rules

When your grandchildren come to your place, you need to respect their parents' rules about behaviour and discipline but you should also be confident enough to let them know that at your place, your rules apply. If you don't want your grandchildren to climb on the bed with their shoes on, or to use your lounge suite as a trampoline, just make it clear to them, kindly but firmly, that this isn't allowed at your place.

If you and your spouse have a rule that you don't eat in front of television, but actually eat together and talk to each other, that can still be the rule when the grandchildren come. The important things about rules are that they should be consistent and that they should not make life miserable. Rules provide a framework that helps children to know how far they can go and within which limitations they can enjoy themselves. Rules provide a degree of security because they are consistent.

A paediatric colleague of mine was a young father in Boston during the 1960s at a time when many parents were reluctant to discipline their children because of the popular view that it could 'interfere with them developing to their full potential'. He'd be invited to his friends' places for dinner, only to find the toddlers running wild and their parents seemingly unable to control them. He would then just pick the toddlers up firmly, take them to their room, read them a bedtime story and tuck them into bed. Then he could enjoy the dinner party and so could the parents. Why did it work? Because these children really wanted someone to take control of them, to help them to understand the limits and to do it in a way they enjoyed.

So don't be afraid to have a few consistent rules at your place. Rules about things children can't do also have to go with things that are fun to them to do. If you have lots of activities planned and if mealtimes are fun, they won't have time to even want to climb on the bed in their shoes, trampoline on the lounge or watch TV while eating. If your rules are too harsh and if they aren't combined with fun and interesting things to do, you'll soon find that they don't come to visit you very often.

An ethical dilemma

You want to be supportive of the parents and for them to have the special joy which comes from seeing their children learn new things. This can present a minor ethical dilemma if you are doing quite a lot of the child care as you may be the first to see a new milestone reached.

Think of this: you are minding your nine-month-old grandson. You place him on a rug on the floor and you later notice that he's got up on his hands and knees, swayed back and forth a little, placed one hand forward, then moved the opposite knee forward, then the other hand and so on. Lo and behold, he's crawling! What do you do?

Do you immediately phone Mum and Dad to tell them the good news? But then you're the one that saw it happen and they haven't had the joy of seeing their son start to crawl. Or do you just keep quiet, knowing that he'll do it again when he's back with them so that they can see him achieve this milestone and phone you with the exciting news? At which point, of course, you show surprise and delight. There is no rule about this, but it's worth thinking about how you'd react.

FAMILY GATHERINGS

Sometimes we may have fantasies about a big, happy, extended family, where everyone gets on with each other famously, even the cousins, and where we as the patriarch and matriarch preside, radiating good will and wisdom. If you come from a large, happy, cohesive family, there is a good chance that this may occur, but if you didn't have it before, just becoming grandparents isn't likely to make it happen all of a sudden. It is better to work toward harmony by honesty and tact in handling 'rough patches' than glossing over any disagreements and 'pretending' that all is well and 'we're just one big happy family'.

This situation is more common than you think. One November, the mother of one of my young patients told me that she dreaded Christmas because everyone was expected to bring slices of their Christmas cake for the other adults to taste. The family matriarch, being slightly deaf, would comment in a loud voice about how some of the women in the family could cook better than others. My patient's mother said that her Christmas cake usually turned out to be the type where the fruit gravitated to the bottom with the cake mixture sitting on the top. She knew she was a pretty good mum, but she also knew that she wasn't a very good cook and found the whole experience, particularly the comments on the quality of her effort, humiliating. This had nothing at all to do with her child's illness and the reason for their visit, but she seemed to want to chat, so we discussed a few options.

It was May the next year before I saw them again. Her son was doing well but that wasn't why she was elated. She told me how in December she had decided to let all the family know that she wouldn't be cooking a Christmas cake that year. Instead, at the Christmas gathering she surprised them all with a magnificent Christmas decoration to be the table centrepiece. She had always been good at craft and so decided to play to her strength. It was a great success, lots of 'oohs' and 'aahs'. The matriarch was particularly impressed. Slices of Christmas cake were still tasted, but for her, the tension had evaporated and Christmas gatherings were fun again.

There is also another ingredient in the family gathering and that's the other set of grandparents. Both sets of grandparents might get on very well, but they are likely to also have extended families of their own and will have obligations to the other members of their family as well as to their child who just happened to have married into your family.

It's worth working out family obligations for special events well in advance. Occasions where the new grandchild is the focus, such as a christening or a birthday, are easy. Usually everyone is invited and the family, including the in-laws, can get together. Christmas and similar occasions are more difficult, especially if you also have your own parents to consider. It's hard to be in several places at the same time! Some grandparents solve this by rotation: they spend Christmas day with different family members each year and catch up with the others at another time during the Christmas holiday period.

Don't fall into the trap of wanting to be your grandchild's 'favourite' grandparents, particularly if it involves trying to be the grandparents who can give the most expensive gifts. It's not worth getting involved in this sort of thing. Your importance as a grandparent isn't measured by how much you can spend. Be generous when you are able, but be sensitive and don't over-do it. Remember that you'll want your grandchildren to love you because of who you are, not because of what you can buy.

If you get on well with the other set of grandparents you can show your unity occasionally by pooling resources at birthdays and at Christmas time to give a combined, perhaps somewhat more grand, gift from both sets of grandparents. That's really showing solidarity.

RIVALRY BETWEEN GRANDCHILDREN

Don't become involved in this if you want to get on well with the parents. You might feel closer to one, or a couple, of your grandchildren than you do to the others. You might think they are more like you, or perhaps that they have greater potential, or that they may just be stunningly cute. It's not unusual to feel preferences, but just make sure they remain as feelings only, as it can be disastrous for family relationships to let feelings such as these show. Instead, work on getting to know your other grandchildren better. You may be surprised at how they will increasingly captivate you.

Each grandchild needs to be treated as a unique, special person, even though they will have different talents, personalities and even shortcomings. Children are very aware of differences and sensitive to any preferential treatment. So it's not clever to brag to one of your grandchildren about how clever or athletic one of your other grandchildren may be. They all need and respond to encouragement and praise. Remember Dr Brazelton's technique.

Do you remember how many photographs you took of your first child and how carefully you filled in the events of her life in the baby book? With subsequent children, the baby book was less likely to be completed and the individual photographs became less. It's a bit like that with grandchildren. Sometimes the first ones get most of the attention. But all of the grandchildren will learn to count. When they come to your place they will notice if there are four photographs of grandchild number one on display, three of grandchild number two and only one of grandchild number three— particularly if they happen to be grandchild number three.

Grandchildren like to see their photographs on display as well as photos of their cousins and other family members. They get a kick out of photos of their parents when they were children. You can buy frames that will hold a number of photographs to make sure that everyone is included. Some grandparents have a photograph wall or a special area where family photos are on display. You can also buy photo holders that can flip over from one photo to the other so that different grandchildren can be on display at different times.

TRAPS TO AVOID

If we want to enhance the relationship with our grandchildren's parents, we need to give grandparenting activities priority, be supportive and not critical and consider what we can bring to the relationship for the parents and for the grandchildren. It may be our time. It may be our wisdom and experience. It may be financial assistance. It may be reliability and stability. It may be a combination of these or it may be other things.

We also need to avoid doing dumb things. If we want to keep the relationship healthy, here are some tips on things to avoid. Don't:

- interfere when your children are reprimanding your grandchild
- compete with the parents for your grandchildren's affection
- make demands on your children that they can't meet; for example, expecting them to visit you at a particular time on a regular day
- address most of your advice and comments about parenting to your own child, practically ignoring the other parent
- make your children feel guilty if they forget (or omit) to do something you had expected or requested. Guilt and insecurity are common. We don't need to reinforce these feelings. We need to counter them with encouragement and praise
- turn up at their place unannounced. For all you know, they might be in bed trying to make another grandchild. Your arrival will spoil it. That's what telephones are for.

3

A Child Development Refresher Course

Grandparents know a lot about child development. After all, we raised our own children. But at times, we were so busy that, although we noticed that they *were* developing we didn't always have time to notice *how* they developed.

The way children develop hasn't really changed, but since we brought up our children a lot has been learned about how it occurs, and even more has been learned about the amazing complexity of the infant brain.

Who of us can clearly remember something that happened in our first year? Our second year? It's a bit of a mystery to us. Our parents have told us some of the cute things we did when we were babies. We've seen photographs. But we don't have a clear memory of these times. Yet in our first year we learnt far more than in any other year of our life. That's not a misprint. *In our first year we learnt far more than in any other year of our life.*

What is the basis of this seemingly preposterous claim? In the early 1970s the study of infant development took off, partly because the video-recorder and then the computer allowed developmental psychologists to record and observe infants and to carefully analyse what they had observed. Then, in the 1990s, brain-imaging techniques and advances in neurobiology gave new information about how the infant's brain develops. It was pretty amazing stuff.

Think about it. Children used to be (and often still are) defined by the things they couldn't do and the things they didn't know, a sort of defective adult. But now we know that children are like young scientists, noting how we, or objects, react when they do something and modifying their response and behaviour accordingly.

Of course there have always been experts who have had opinions about children. In the early twentieth century, psychoanalyst Sigmund Freud and the behavioural scientist Robert Skinner had lots to say about children. But neither Freud nor Skinner actually observed them. Freud relied largely on inferences he drew from the behaviour and the dreams of neurotic adults. Skinner relied on inferences from slightly less neurotic laboratory rats. Neither took the time to carefully and systematically observe what children actually did and how they used these behaviours to learn.

Once people started to closely observe how children developed, we really began to learn about them. Yet there is still a folk wisdom about babies—that they can't see at birth; that they can't recognise their parents—and that basically they have only four abilities: to drink, to sleep, to cry and to excrete, the latter sometimes from three different places all at the same time. But observant mothers know that this folklore seems to be wrong about their own babies. They know that their babies can see them and recognise them and react to them.

WHAT WE KNOW NOW

If you show a newborn baby a picture of a human face and a picture just made up of patterns and record the baby's eye movements to see which picture she spends the most time looking at, she'll spend more time looking towards the face.

Boys and girls are different from birth. And I don't just mean in their dangly bits. One study done in Boston in the 1990s was designed to look at what day-old girls and day-old boys preferred to look at. The babies were shown a picture of a friendly face or a mechanical object to see which picture they preferred to spend more time looking at. The result? You've guessed it. The day-old baby girls spent more time looking at the friendly face. The boys liked the face too, but they spent more time than the girls looking at the mechanical object.

Babies just a few days old will respond more to their mother's voice than to a stranger's. This applies to boys as well as girls. They also have an awareness of parts of their body they haven't even seen. If you open your mouth in front of a baby, she'll open her mouth in response. Now poke your tongue out and watch the baby's response. You'll see her little tongue come forward too, imitating what she has seen. Babies can do this from the first few weeks of life. How can they do it? There are no mirrors in the womb. It's just dark and wet in there. How does the baby know that her tongue is inside her mouth and the thing she is looking at in the adult is also a mouth and a tongue and that she can imitate the movement she has seen?

From an early age babies learn to behave from watching how their parents (and their grandparents) behave. Imagine this: a baby is watching an adult who has two boxes in front of him. The adult peeks inside one box and then looks at the baby with an expression of disgust on his face. The adult then peeks inside the other box and then looks at the baby with an expression of delight. He then pushes the two boxes over to the baby. What does the baby do? He won't open the box that made the adult look disgusted, but he happily looks into the box that made the adult look happy. Right from the early months, babies learn how to behave by watching us. This has important implications for how they turn out.

In one further example, researchers tied one end of a ribbon to a baby's foot and the other end to a mobile hanging above the baby's cot. The baby quickly worked out that if he kicked his leg, the mobile would move. They then took the mobile away. After a week they hung the mobile back up but didn't tie it to the baby's foot. What did the baby do? He immediately started kicking the leg that the mobile had been attached to previously.

But in some of these experiments, after a week, they replaced the mobile with one that looked quite different. What did the baby do now? This time the baby just looked at the mobile but didn't kick his leg. Even at just a couple of months of age, babies can understand cause and effect—'If I kick my leg, the mobile moves'—

and can remember events—'Hey, that mobile's back. I'll kick my leg to make it move'—and shapes—'That's a nice mobile, but it's different from the one which moved when I kicked my leg. I guess there's no point in kicking.'

WHAT ABOUT LANGUAGE?

Language is complex and subtle. It means a lot more than just knowing a large number of words. When we listen to someone talk, we sort out the ambiguities, the tone of voice and all of the other subtleties. Most of the time we get it right. If we don't, the results can be disastrous.

We know that the same three words don't necessarily mean the same thing if the words aren't in the same order. 'Andy loves Michelle' doesn't necessarily mean 'Michelle loves Andy', much to Andy's disappointment.

By the time a child is of kindergarten age, she will have mastered almost all of the complexities of her particular language. Even if she still can't articulate all the words clearly, she can certainly understand them, as well as most of the subtleties of speech. If she lives in a multilingual family, she will have mastered the complexities of several languages, all with apparent ease.

So when do babies talk? The answer is that they learn many of the elements of speech well before they start saying words. After about four years of age, our ability to quickly and effortlessly learn another language and speak it like a native becomes largely lost.

NEW INFORMATION ABOUT BABIES' BRAINS

Children have an innate drive to learn and to explore. They observe, create a theory, do an experiment and then perhaps modify their theory as a result of what they learn. Children experiment by watching our reactions to what they do and modifying their behaviour accordingly. You could say that they are the young scientists and we adults are the laboratory rats they are observing.

How can babies, so small and so helpless, be so smart? Did you notice that your children and your grandchildren had relatively large heads in relation to the size of their bodies when they were born? At birth, all babies have relatively large heads. Why? It's not just to make childbirth painful. Recent research has shown that the baby's head is large because it contains pretty well all of the neurons (brain cells) that they'll ever need. A baby's brain has about 100 billion neurons. That's about the same as the number of stars in the Milky Way.

Babies' brains are incredibly busy. After birth, as experiences such as sounds, smells, sights and touch flood into the brain, the brain cells fire off rapidly to make connections with each other. These connections set up a complex pattern of brain wiring and as these experiences are repeated, the brain lays down permanent connections that consolidate all of the things that the baby is learning.

By two years, the child's brain is consuming as much energy as an adult brain. Now I know you can think of adults whose brains don't seem to consume any energy at all, but think of normal adults, like you and your children. By three years, the child's brain is twice as active as an adult brain. This high level of brain activity continues until about nine years and then starts to decline to adult levels. So the early years are important for learning, for teaching and for influencing behaviour. And grandparents can play a valuable role here.

The early years are a crucial time for children. It's a time when development is vulnerable but is also robust. You can probably think of people who have done well despite having had a terrible childhood. They are sometimes held up as examples to follow. Some children can indeed do well despite poor childhood experiences, but they are in the minority. Most who have adverse childhood experiences don't do nearly as well as they would have done otherwise. Good early childhood experiences set a baseline for learning, behaviour and health throughout life.

WHAT CHILDREN NEED

Armed with this new knowledge about the amazing infant brain and the importance of the early years, what can we grandparents, who may have more disposable income than our children, do to help? Should we buy expensive educational toys, offer to pay for infant stimulation classes, suggest that we sign them up for some child development program we find on the internet? Here is a warning: be very suspicious of programs, particularly the expensive ones, which offer a formula for making normal children smarter. Babies are already very smart. We've just seen that.

Infants are very good at getting the information they need. They are designed to learn in the real world. They learn best by playing with people who love them, and that includes their grandparents. From a baby's point of view, being taught and being cared for can't be separated. Babies learn when we talk with them, cuddle them, make funny faces, laugh with them, pay attention to them and value them. What is needed much more than expensive programs is time to be with infants and toddlers. Time to talk with them, play with them and just hang out with them and let them hang out with us. Grandparents often have this time. So, if the child's parents are happy, it's good to be part of the team that helps your grandchildren's development and relationships and where you can also be a good role model for them. And it keeps us young too.

MEMORABLE MILESTONES

Here is a quick reminder of some of the developmental milestones during childhood. Just remember they are for the average baby. Some babies reach some milestones sooner, others reach them later. There is a wide variation in normal development. Just because a milestone is delayed, doesn't mean there is a problem. But it might. The more delayed, the more likely there is to be a problem, particularly if the delay is in several areas.

The newborn
As we've seen, these cute little creatures can already see, hear, know about their own bodies and have preferences. Their hands are closed most of the time but they'll involuntarily grasp your finger if you place it in their palm.

Six to eight weeks

They can now lift their head when lying on their stomach. Their hands are now open for most of the time. They smile back when you smile and talk with them. They make lots of cooing and gooing sounds which make you feel all cooey and gooey inside. They follow intently with their eyes.

Three months

By three months, the baby will reach out towards an object she wants, such as a toy, but usually can't grasp it voluntarily. Of course she'll be able to hold it if you place it in her hand, but that's different. At this age, the grasp is just a reflex, not something babies can control. They get excited when they see things they recognise and enjoy, such as mum's breast, or their bath and they may squeal with delight. They now start to turn their head towards soft sounds and their vocalisation becomes more tuneful.

Six months

By six months, most babies can roll from their back to their front and from their front onto their back. This means that they can also roll off beds and change tables, so if you're minding them, never leave them unattended, even for a moment. Some can sit unsupported for a few moments, although it may be another month before they can sit steadily without toppling over.

They can now grasp objects they reach for and may transfer toys from one hand to the other. They test everything they pick up by sticking it straight into their mouth, a habit that persists until 12 months, by which time they have presumably worked out what tastes good and what doesn't.

They have been laughing since about four months and they enjoy looking at themselves in the mirror. If you take away a toy they are playing with, they may become upset. They may mimic sounds they hear, such as a cough.

Around this age many babies show a fear of strangers. If someone they don't recognise offers to take them out of their parent's arms for a kiss or a cuddle, they may look frightened, cry and hang on to their parent for dear life. This can be quite

...roll off beds or change tables

unnerving for the poor adult who offers to hold the baby. If, for some reason, you haven't been able to see your grandchild for a few weeks, she may take one look at you and scream blue murder. Don't worry, it's only temporary.

Nine months

This is an exciting period of development and great fun. They can now crawl. They can stand holding onto something for support and in the next month or so they'll be able to use the lounge or a chair to pull themselves up into the standing position.

They have learned that things still exist even if they can't see them and so will look for hidden objects and be able to play peekaboo. They'll play pat-a-cake, shout out to attract your attention and react to praise.

Although they can't say any clear words, they can understand many of the words that they hear, perhaps 100 to 200, and they file these words away in their brain, ready for the time when they have enough tongue and mouth coordination to say them.

Their rather clumsy grip has now been replaced by a nice pincer grasp where small objects can be picked up using the forefinger and thumb. It's a great time, but it's also a time when they can be a mobile disaster waiting to happen: they can crawl towards small, dangerous or unpleasant objects (buttons, peanuts, pins, dead blowflies and cockroaches), pick them up neatly with their newly acquired pincer grip and automatically pop them into the mouth where the object could be swallowed or inhaled. Constant supervision is more important than ever now.

12 months

For the last month or so they have been waving goodbye, clapping hands and perhaps saying, 'Mumma' and 'Dadda', and hopefully 'Pappa' and 'Nanna', or whatever names you have chosen. They have stopped saying, 'Dadda' to anyone they see, such as the milkman or the dog, and now say it just for their dad.

They've been able to walk around furniture and now they can walk with you holding one hand, if they aren't already walking alone. Their speech, which still sounds like a Martian dialect, is loud and vigorous and although they can only say a few words, they understand many hundreds, another good reason for not swearing in front of them.

They know their name and will turn to it when you call them and they can drink confidently from a baby cup. That habit of testing everything by putting it into the mouth has just about gone. If you give them pencil and paper they will scribble and if they are sitting in a highchair they'll take great delight in throwing things onto the floor. This is fine when it's just toys but a bit of a problem when it's braised lamb with gravy and vegetables.

18 months

Now they can walk confidently, negotiate corners smoothly and are starting to run. They can climb up onto a chair or lounge and can jump. Jumping on the lounge is likely to become their new, favourite sport. They are showing hand preference (about one person in fifteen is left-handed) and can stack three or four blocks on top of each other. They can name two or three parts of their body, will obey some simple commands (if they feel like it) and may indicate when they are using their bowel or bladder. They may use up to 20 recognisable words, but of course they can understand many more. They can use a spoon reasonably well, although sometimes it's upside down by the time it gets to their mouth. At other times they just prefer to use it as a hammer, rather than as a culinary utensil.

They start to look at pictures in books (a great opportunity for grandparents to introduce them to books), but usually can't yet turn pages one at a time. They love to explore, will open drawers and cupboards and like to drag around their favourite cuddly toy wherever they go. They may start to become negative as they test their environment and test their parents, a foretaste of more negative behaviour over the next twelve months.

Two years

They are now physically quite skilful and can run, kick a ball and stack five to seven blocks on top of each other. They have lots of words, perhaps up to 50, and will have some two- and three-word phrases. Pronouns start to be used and they can often say their name. Their interest in picture books increases and they can turn the pages one at a time.

They may be toilet trained although there will still be some 'accidents', particularly when they are immersed in an interesting game. Most are not yet dry by night. They can name a few toys and know four or five parts of their body. They can take off some of their clothes and they start to play alongside other children. Their behaviour can be quite negative. This is also the age when fantasy play starts and it's a delight to watch.

The terrible twos

Suddenly your cute, compliant grandchild starts to be negative. 'No' becomes his favourite word. He has a tantrum if he is frustrated. What has happened? The terrible twos, which may often start from eighteen months, are just part of normal development. They are a clash between a two-year-old's need to understand us and to live in peace and harmony with us.

Two year olds are always testing their parents and their grandparents when they get the chance. It's not because they are naughty or bad, rather, it's because they want to learn how we react in different situations. It's not that ornament you told him not to touch that really interests him, it's your reaction when he touches it that he really wants to learn about.

It's this drive, this passion to learn, that makes two year olds want to try out everything, particularly forbidden things. And like adults, they'll become grumpy and negative and get the sulks if they are frustrated or don't get their own way.

In the process of all of this exploratory, testing behaviour, the two year old, if he survives, learns plenty. He learns about how things work, but much more importantly, by observing how we react, he learns about human behaviour and how people relate to each other. It's another example of the young scientist at work. He grabs something, we react: he notes our reaction, learns from it and modifies his behaviour as a result. Of course, he might learn that our reaction is so much fun—such as being bribed not to touch something or being distracted with something which is really interesting—that he'll touch it again and again just to have our reaction repeated. That's why putting our favourite objects out of sight and out of bounds and ignoring difficult behaviour is often much more effective than reacting in a way which might even reinforce negative behaviour.

Three years

By this age they can ride a tricycle, draw a circle and build a tower of eight or nine blocks. Their expressive language has taken off so that they now have a wide vocabulary, can give their full name, and talk in three- to five-word sentences, including lots of questions. Their parents will understand their speech better than strangers and the more time the grandparents spend talking with them, the more they will be able to understand what they say.

They can often count to ten, understand prepositions and may know some nursery rhymes. They can wash and dry their hands and face, can undress themselves, can get dressed with help and thankfully, they are starting to become less negative.

Their fantasy play is now rich and varied. They like to incorporate toys and adults, including grandparents, into their fantasy play. To be asked by a three year old to get under the table with her because she is making a house there, is one of life's great privileges. You just have to be able to bend your knees and back well enough to enjoy it.

Four years

Their physical skills are now likely to outclass some of the physical skills of their grandparents. They can hop on one foot and run fast.

They can do up buttons, unless they've been raised in a family where everything joins together with Velcro, can draw a cross, know the primary colours and attempt to draw a person which is instantly recognisable by family members but by few others. Their language is rich. They can give their address. They love to ask questions and like repetitions and rituals—'Read that again, Pappa' after you have just finished reading *The Hungry Caterpillar* for the fifth consecutive time. Their fantasy play becomes even richer and more imaginative and they don't mind asking Baby Boomers to be part of it.

Five years

They can now skip, may be able to outrun their grandparents, can draw a person comprising six or more parts, can dress themselves without help, speak fluently and understand the rules of play. They are now ready for school.

All grandparents think that their grandchildren are incredibly intelligent. It may be just because it's the first time we've really watched a child develop. With our own children, we were too busy looking after them, shopping for them, pulling them apart when they fought and cleaning up after them to actually notice how they learned and developed.

Can milestones help predict intelligence? Not really. Some children achieve milestones earlier than others, but this doesn't necessarily make them any smarter. Milestones are more useful for predicting developmental delay or developmental disability. If a child is well behind the average in a range of milestones, there may well be a problem and a specialist check-up is needed. The parents would usually have noticed this and you won't want to interfere, although it may be worth mentioning in a concerned way.

It's much harder for milestones to predict high intelligence. The best predictors of high intelligence are curiosity, good concentration and rich, early language development. But it's wise for grandparents not to make predictions or odious comparisons.

DIFFERENCES IN DEVELOPMENT

Children differ in a whole range of ways, in their personalities, their activity levels and their rate of development.

Temperament

You would have noticed that some adults are calm and placid while others always seem anxious. Some of us are lethargic and laidback, while others of us are always on the go. Is this a result of how we were brought up or is it in our genes? If we think about our own children we'll remember that they may have each had different temperaments which seemed to have been there right from birth, yet we reared them in much the same way.

Although parents have always known that babies are born with different temperaments, it wasn't until the 1950s that psychologists documented the different types of temperament. Some are more active than others. There are the wrigglers, the climbers, the early walkers, the explorers and the fidgeters. Some are very adaptable; things change and they don't bother much. They tend to be peaceful and unflappable in contrast to the infant who doesn't like change and becomes upset whenever the routine changes.

Some have a happy disposition and always smile, while others don't seem to be all that joyful. Some children have the ability to concentrate, while others have short attention spans and become distracted by the slightest little thing. Some children love new experiences, new places, different foods and new acquaintances, while others don't like change, won't explore and don't like to be separated from their parents. Some are easy to soothe and comfort when they are upset, while those with different temperaments can be really hard to console.

Of course there is a spectrum between these various extremes. No one temperament type is 'good' or 'bad', or even particularly related to intelligence. That's the way we were born, so we shouldn't be surprised if our grandchildren differ from each other in temperament, differ from our own children (although you'll often see family resemblances in temperaments) and differ from our idealised idea of the perfect grandchild.

Temperament can be influenced and modified by how children are brought up, but the basic temperament is in-built. Understanding differences in temperament helps us to understand why one grandchild is different from the other and may stop us blaming the parent (we always think it's the parent who is not our child) for any temperament characteristics that don't fit with what we'd really like.

The Australian Temperament Project has sound information on this subject. This particular study has been following over 2000 Australian families for 21 years, looking at differences in temperament in the early years and outcomes related to temperament in later life. Information is available from the Australian Institute of Family Studies, telephone (03) 9214 7888 or go to their website at www.aifs.gov.au.

Boys and girls

Boys and girls differ in more than just their anatomy; they often have different temperaments. As we mentioned earlier, newborn baby boys spend more time looking at mechanical patterns than do baby girls. Baby boys are often more physical, while girls often spend more time looking and listening.

There was a time in the 1970s when some gurus taught that there was no difference between little girls and little boys and that they should all be treated in exactly the same way, with the same toys and same attitudes, to avoid any male–female stereotypes and role modelling. It didn't work. The little boys still got together and wrestled with each other and played wild and adventurous games, and the little girls spent more time talking and playing mothering games.

These days girls can do anything boys can do in terms of jobs and careers and they can often do it better than the boys. In most cases, however, whatever their role or career, most boys still like to be boys and most girls like to be girls.

THE IMPORTANCE OF PLAY

Play is the way children learn. We play when we aren't working, but for children play is their work. They don't play to relax as we do, they play to learn. Play is a child's unique way of experimenting and learning. Play is the way they acquire their physical skills, balance, coordination and muscle strength. Playing with other children helps them to develop social skills such as cooperation and sharing. We shouldn't be surprised that they don't have these skills straightaway.

Grandparents can be part of a child's play. We can participate in their imaginative play when they invite us, or we can even initiate imaginative play with them. There is no point in being a stuffy, staid, boring grandparent when you could be a hunter, pretending to camp in the backyard with your grandchildren to spot some passing elephants, or a princess decorating her newly acquired castle.

Sometimes we confuse play with expensive toys. Toys are an important part of play, but toys which can be incorporated into imaginative games are often much more fun than ones which are large and expensive but which lose their attraction after a few days, or even a few minutes.

What children need the most is *time* to play as their lives are often so busy with programmed activity. This is why a visit to the grandparents can be a time when they can just play, with or without our involvement and can have fun.

DISCIPLINE

Grandparents won't normally be involved in discipline, that's one of the great advantages of being a grandparent, but if you are given responsibility for some of the child care, and with that some of the discipline, here are some hints.

One problem with discipline is that many people think discipline means smacking. There is a whole range of disciplinary measures. The best are through teaching and role modelling. The origin of the word 'discipline' relates more to instruction and training than to hitting.

Other methods of discipline include the use of time-out, withdrawal of privileges, reinforcing good behaviour and ignoring bad behaviour, so that the child does not get attention because of undesirable behaviour. Smacking, if it has any place at all, is a low in the hierarchy of effective disciplines. In fact, several recent studies have shown that while smacking does have an immediate, short-term effect, in the longer term the undesirable behaviour doesn't stop and may even become worse.

Of course this doesn't mean that children can be let loose to do whatever they like. Children like to have clear boundaries for their behaviour. The most important aspects of discipline are that the rules have to be reasonable and in line with the child's developmental abilities. They have to be consistent and need to be agreed on and applied consistently by all who look after the child. This can be a testing time for grandparents as you don't make the rules. These are made by your children and as grandparents we have to respect them.

TOILET TRAINING

Another nice thing about being a grandparent is that someone else does the toilet training. Children achieve bowel and bladder control at different ages. Bowel control usually comes first. Most toddlers can indicate when they are about to urinate and can hold on for a few moments, unless of course they are absorbed in a game and then they may just let it happen.

Girls, being superior in so many ways, tend to become toilet trained a little earlier.

('What!' male readers may say. 'Girls are superior in many ways! Do you really mean this?' Yes chaps, sadly for us, it's true. Fewer girls die in the first few years of life because they are better equipped for survival than we mere males. Many of the developmental milestones come earlier in girls, particularly language and social skills, as is evident throughout childhood and teenage years. Females have fewer problems related to violence, alcohol and drug abuse and coronary heart disease. These are just some of the facts which explain why females live longer than males.)

Sitting perched on a toilet can be a pretty scary thing for a small two year old. It's the same as an adult being perched, legs dangling, on a toilet bowl almost 2 metres high and a metre across, easily large enough to fall into. A child's toilet seat that fits inside the regular toilet seat helps get the size right and a plastic footrest placed under the child's feet helps him with that extra push sometimes needed when passing poo.

By three years, most children will only need to wear a nappy at night. About half will be dry at night by four years, although 20 per cent of five year olds and 7 per cent of seven year olds still wet the bed, so a waterproof sheet on the mattress is useful for overnight stays. It's a little known fact, but about 1 to 2 per cent of adults, including grandparents, wet the bed, so it's not all that unusual.

SLEEPING

Remember, infants spend much of their time sleeping. The newborn may spend 18 to 20 hours per day asleep, which explains why your new grandchild is likely to be asleep when you go to visit her. Six-month-old infants average 16 to 18 hours' sleep and even the one year old sleeps 14 to 15 hours.

If you go to visit your grandchild and she is asleep, you may feel a touch disappointed that you won't get a cuddle. However, this is a chance you may never have had time for with your own children, to enjoy watching a sleeping baby. Just sit quietly and look at her. In some stages of sleep she will be motionless, with regular breathing. At other times, the breathing will be irregular, her hands may move a little and you'll notice her eyes fluttering under her closed eyelids. She'll be dreaming in this sleep state, probably about a large breast and a good feed.

The newborn will have five or six sleep cycles throughout the day, waking to feed, to look around and to listen and then falling back to sleep until the next meal. What a life. Even in retirement it doesn't get this good.

By one year, most children just have two sleep cycles, the afternoon nap and the evening sleep, a little like their grandparents aspire to each weekend.

By four years, children sleep on average 12 hours a day. By five years most children have outgrown the need for an afternoon nap. By eight or nine years, the need for sleep is less but it varies a lot between children. Some seem to get by on six to seven hours, perhaps needing less sleep than their parents, while others still need 12 to 13 hours. Both of these examples are within the normal range.

It's not unusual for children to wake in the night during the first two years. Most children will wake several times every night although, unless they are sleeping in their parents' room, their parents will not be aware of most of these brief waking episodes.

EATING AND DRINKING

Even though grandparents have successfully fed and raised their own children, it's still common for grandparents to worry that their grandchildren aren't eating enough, or getting enough of the right foods. Again, it's important to remember that is not our decision what they eat and, if we're really honest, our eating patterns may not be all that healthy either.

The basic rule is that if a child is growing normally, he'll be getting enough to eat, even if he refuses meals at times. While our idea of fun might be to sit down to a nine-course degustation menu, spread over three hours, the toddler's idea of fun is to run around, play, experiment and explore and not be stuck in a highchair for too long. Children also like to experiment with food, to see how far they can throw it and to watch it squish through their fingers. They may wonder why you don't leap at the chance to accept the tasty morsel they take out of their mouth to offer you.

This is all part of their play and learning about life. By the time they are taking their first girlfriend to a restaurant for a date, their manners will have transformed. If they haven't, the romance could be short-lived.

We remember the times when children don't eat, but tend to forget when they do. If you could put all the food your grandchild consumed in a year into one big pile in the middle of your lounge room, mix it all up and then divide it into 365 portions, you'd find that each portion was pretty close to the normal daily dietary requirement, even though you and the grandchild's parents may have despaired at times during the year.

People are much more conscious of the importance of good nutrition than when we were children or even when we were young parents. As you know, good eating habits start early and set the stage for eating patterns in adult life. So it's most likely that the way your children eat and feed their grandchildren will reflect the early influence you had on their lives. A sobering thought.

It's worth reminding ourselves about the basic aims for good nutrition which should start in infancy: reduce fat intake; cut down on salty foods; do not offer too many highly refined or sweet foods, but serve up plenty of vegetables, fruit, pasta, rice, potatoes (not fried) and breads. And even if you don't want to, or can't, influence your children and grandchildren to follow these dietary habits, it won't hurt to follow them yourself.

Does this mean that you can't ever take your grandchild to a fast food outlet even if it's convenient for you or because your grandchild would like it? The theory says 'no', but the reality is that although eating at a fast food outlet may be inevitable, try not to make it a habit. Make it a rare event if at all, and don't build it up as something special. If your grandchildren think that the most exciting thing about visiting your place is that they'll also be visiting a fast-food outlet, it suggests a pretty slim repertoire of ways to entertain and enjoy your grandchildren. (See chapters 4 and 5 for some ideas on how to entertain them.)

To watch a child grow, explore, learn, develop language, make friends, develop empathy and grow into a reasonably well-adjusted adult is pretty good. We had a taste of it when we raised our own children. That experience has primed us to be blown away as we watch the process unfold in our grandchildren.

4

Getting Along with the Grandchildren

Why do grandchildren love their grandparents? It can't be because they are fascinated by people with grey hair (or absent hair), wrinkles and a spreading midriff. In fact, not all grandchildren do love their grandparents. Some have no time for them or interest in them, and some grandparents have little interest in their grandchildren. It wasn't meant to be like that when the new grandchild arrived. But like a good marriage, it takes some work to be a good grandparent. If we want long-term, secure and rewarding relationships with our grandchildren, we'll need to do a little work, or have a little fun depending on how you look at it, to develop the relationship.

WHAT YOU CAN OFFER

While there are lots of different types of grandparents, what a good grandparent can provide comes under four broad headings: unconditional love, a role model, security and stability, adviser and counsellor, and a sense of family continuity.

Unconditional love
Good parents love their children unconditionally. They may not always approve of what they do. They may even hate some of the

things they do, but they love them through thick and thin, through good times and bad.

They love their toddler when he says his first word and they still love him when he drops the car keys down the toilet. They love their teenagers when they can talk with them adult to adult and share ideas and they still love them when they borrow the new family car, leave the handbrake off and find that it rolls into a brick wall. Parents love their children just because they are their children. They love them for who they are, not for what they can do. There are no conditions on this type of love.

Grandparents can also provide unconditional love for their grandchildren. This doesn't mean letting them always do exactly what they like and tolerating absolutely everything. Sure, we might disapprove at times. Our children may even ask us to present a united front with them to express disapproval for some unpleasant habit or behaviour. But we'll still love them and value them, not for what they do or don't do, but because they are our grandchildren. It's good to let them know this. Let them know that you're proud to be their grandparent.

When I was about six years old, I went to play with a boy a few houses up the street. He was crying. He told me that he had just been punished for swearing. I didn't even know what swearing was, so he gave me a comprehensive list of words which he said were fun to use, but which mustn't ever be said in front of your parents. I heeded his advice, swore only at school and, being a show-off, swore with vigour and emphasis. Of course it wasn't long before someone told my parents. They expressed their disappointment and I tearfully promised never to swear again. They also said I'd have to tell my grandfather, who was a clergyman, about my behaviour when we next visited him. My grandfather combined his clerical role with compassion, humour and generosity.

With some anxiety I entered his study. He said, 'I hear you've been swearing.'

'Yes, Grandpa,' I replied.

'Well, I'm sure you won't be doing that any more. Have this.' And he handed me a small parcel. I'd been collecting a series of sporting cards and was keen to build the collection. Unbeknown to me, he'd been collecting some to give me. The packet contained a wonderful array of cards; not a reward for swearing and not a reward for promising to stop swearing. He accepted me as I was, showed that he trusted me and gave me the gift I really wanted. Love with no conditions.

A role model

Grandparents can be good role models. Little children are great mimics. This is the beginning of following a role model. As they become older, they'll become more aware of your good qualities as well as your bad qualities. Many teenagers go through a phase of thinking their parents aren't all that smart and that they know absolutely nothing about the modern world. At this stage they often unconsciously look around for other role models. A trusted and reliable grandparent can be one of those role models. I don't mean that they'll want to be like you physically, heaven forbid! But if they have come to love you and respect you because you've always been fair, consistent, kind, reliable and available, there is a good chance that some of these qualities will brush off onto them.

It's probably too late for us to start developing these qualities for the first time when our grandchildren become teenagers, but it's worth brushing up on them when the first grandchild arrives. You might also want to add to that list a sense of humour, a reasonable amount of energy and being honest enough to admit you don't know everything and that you make mistakes.

Security and stability

The fact that you are still around and haven't gone totally bonkers is reassuring and part of the sense of security and continuity that develops in families.

Grandparents can help when they are needed—perhaps for babysitting; perhaps to help out in a family crisis; sometimes to help in material ways. You're not part of the nuclear family but you can be an important part of the family: available to give advice, practical help and perhaps occasional financial help in the short term (at least you hope it will be short term). Grandparents can encourage their grandchildren, support them emotionally and let them know that they care about them. Grandparents can help their grandchildren to develop trust because they learn that their grandparents can be trusted and relied upon.

Sometimes serious problems occur which can disrupt the grandchild's world and perhaps badly influence their whole future. This may be divorce or separation of their parents, drug or alcohol abuse, domestic violence or physical and sexual abuse. In those circumstances, grandparents and their home can be the one continuing source of security.

Adviser and counsellor

Another role for grandparents which can continue long after they are unable to climb trees with their grandchildren is that of adviser and counsellor. If the grandparent has always been reliable, fair, consistent and a good listener, that role can continue. You don't have to have all the answers, just listening is enough. In the process, your grandchild seeking guidance will usually work it out for himself. Psychiatrists have known this for along time. They don't have all the answers but they know that much can be accomplished just by being a good listener and letting people talk without judging them.

I remember seeing young Julie, whose parents were both drug addicts. They split up when she was five. Julie's mother had a succession of live-in boyfriends and there was suspicion that Julie had been sexually abused, although this was never proven. The family moved from one lot of rented accommodation to another, sometimes staying in squats. It was a downhill progression. Julie had behavioural problems at school and a couple of times had run away from home briefly. You would have thought that the odds were stacked against Julie making much of her life. What was in her favour was that Julie's grandmother visited her once a week and Julie often spent weekends and school holidays with her grandparents. They noticed that she had a gift for singing and encouraged her musical talents. They were supportive of Julie, gave careful guidance and unconditional love so that despite her poor start, Julie made it through high school, won a music scholarship and is now a music teacher, happy in her job and loved by her students.

One of my role models was a very wise American psychiatrist. When he was in his nineties, I asked him why, in his experience, some children from adverse circumstances did well while others didn't. What explained this difference? He said that those who did well usually had one person, perhaps a different family member, a schoolteacher or a neighbour, who they could trust and rely upon and who became a role model for them. It was these fortunate children who were the survivors. I guess that explains why Julie turned out well.

Family continuity

You are the person who knows the family history, perhaps even some of the family secrets. You were born in the last millennium, over half a century ago. You can remember when colour television arrived. You may even remember when television first came to Australia. If your family wasn't one of the lucky few who could afford one, you may remember going out at night with your parents to stand outside the local electrical shop, along with others from the neighbourhood, to watch the television playing in the shop window.

You know the members of the extended family, past and present. You can tell your grandchildren that you had grandparents too, grandparents who probably lived through World War I or perhaps died in it.

You're the ones who changed the nappies on one of their parents, who fed them and taught them how to get dressed. Children like to know about their family, their cousins and aunts, their origins and their achievements. It gives them a sense of belonging and continuity and grandparents are an important part of this.

A great way to cement yourself into the family history and to give your grandchildren a sense of continuity is to do an oral history with them. This works well with older grandchildren and is a good way for you and your teenage grandchildren to spend time together. They think of the questions (for example, 'Where were you born?', 'Where did you go to school?', 'What did your father do for a job?', 'What games did you play?', 'What were your friends like?' and so on) and then they sit down with you, turn on a recording device, like a tape recorder, and let the conversation flow. You will recall things you thought you'd forgotten. Your grandchildren will learn interesting things about you, particularly how much life has changed and your own children will probably learn a few new things too. Depending on what your life has been like, you may want to combine honesty and frankness with a little tact and discretion.

It's surprising how much comes out in an oral history. There seems to be something about the set questions and the recorder sitting between you that makes discussion easier than at other times. When I did an oral history with my own parents, some quite surprising and rather lovely things came out which were never discussed before. I only wish that when I was a teenager someone had suggested I did oral histories with my grandparents.

SKILLS TO HAVE

Grandparents need a range of skills including a sense of humour, the ability to listen, flexibility as situations change, a willingness to learn from our grandchildren and techniques for remembering all those small, but important details.

A sense of humour

Children have a great sense of humour. By just four months of age they are laughing. They like grandparents who have a sense of humour too. Children also have a sense of the ridiculous, particularly four to six year olds. They like imaginative stories and fantasy play. Sometimes they can believe that their fantasy play is quite serious and important. We grandparents might want to laugh about it with each other when they are not around, but certainly not in front of them.

On the other hand, they like to see and hear about funny things, particularly the slapstick. They like grandparents who laugh with them, rather than at them, and who are prepared to be involved in fantasy play and to do just what the young five year old tells them to do as their role in the game, however undistinguished that may be.

Being a good listener

Children have so much information they want to impart. If we are just happy to listen to them, they'll tell us all sorts of interesting things about their friends, their family (hopefully nothing *too* interesting), their school, shows they've seen on television or stories they've heard. They don't need to be interrogated, something which tends to be unproductive. Just the occasional prompt such as, 'What happened then?' or, 'What did she do after that?' is usually enough to keep the story flowing. They'll love you, just for the time you gave to listen to them.

Occasionally an older grandchild might tell you something important, or even something disturbing which the parents don't know about. What do you do then? It's important to listen without being judgmental, otherwise that will be the last time you'll be told anything important. But it is wise to give guidance and also wise to avoid falling into the trap of lining up with the grandchild against the parents. The stand-up comedian's line, 'Why do grandparents and grandchildren get along so well? Because they're united against a common enemy!' is funny, but not good for enduring relationships. If you've been told something important that their parents need to know, you might consider saying something like, 'Thank you for telling me. This is really important and I'm sure the best thing would be to discuss it with your mum and dad. Do you want me to be with you?'

The next few paragraphs may make you feel a little uncomfortable, but they are important. We know that sexual abuse is common, but we don't like to think it could occur in our own family. What if your grandchild tells you that she (or he, it happens to boys too) has been abused in some way? This is serious. If the alleged abuser is someone outside the family, it's a little easier. There are clear reporting lines in each Australian state, usually to the Department of Community Services or its equivalent.

This is not a problem that can be glossed over in the hope that it won't happen again. In most cases, sexual abuse of children is repetitive and can last for months or years unless action is taken.

Don't play detective; leave that to the experts. Tell your grandchild that this is something that they have to tell their parents with you there to support them if she wishes. And then, perhaps together, you and the parents can let the proper authorities know so that there can be appropriate intervention.

When sexual abuse occurs within the family, the situation is much more complicated. This is a time when you might want to seek advice by calling one of the major children's hospitals in your state. They all have a well-established Child Protection Unit. The relevant authorities will have to be informed, painful as this may be for you and the family. Sadly, life is unlikely to ever be the same again, but it is something you don't really have any choice about if you really care about your grandchild.

'But, don't children make up stories about sexual abuse?' you ask. Well, they do, but only rarely. In a recent large-scale study of over 700 child sex-abuse cases in Canada, there were no false allegations by children, although there were some false allegations made by desperate parents in custody disputes. In another study of over 500 cases from the United States (which I carried out), the rate of false allegations by children was less than 1.5 per cent.

Sexual abuse is a very serious problem which can have a number of long-term adverse consequences. If it does crop up, don't ignore it. Stay calm and get advice from those with expertise in this area.

ADAPTING YOUR STYLE

You'll need to adapt your style as your grandchildren grow older. Crawling around on the floor with them to play lions and tigers or getting them into your bed to play 'there were three in the bed and the middle one said, "Roll over, roll over". So they all rolled over and one fell out' can be fun with a three year old, especially when it's your turn to be the one who rolls out of bed, but not quite as appropriate with a 15-year-old grandchild. That's a good thing, because by the time your grandchildren are 15, you may not be as sprightly as when they were three. By then, crawling around on the floor in imitation of a tiger or rolling out of bed may have lost some of its sparkle.

Older grandchildren are more likely to enjoy a visit to a restaurant, a sporting event, a concert or a movie. The challenge for you will be to enjoy the type of concert or movie they want to go to. It's also an opportunity for you to learn about their world. It's unlikely that your tastes and theirs will coincide, but sharing a real interest in their likes (instead of grumbling about modern music…'no tune'…'too noisy') will open up other avenues which may allow them to talk to you about their ambitions, their hopes and perhaps their fears. That is, providing you are a thoughtful, non-judgmental listener.

LEARNING SOMETHING NEW

Allow your grandchild to teach you something. Young children are natural teachers and delight in showing adults how to do things. If you're having trouble with your computer, or if you haven't mastered the art of sending text messages, your grandchild may be able to set you straight. Then you can email and text-message each other.

You might become involved in helping your grandchild with some school projects, and I don't just mean the one where they have to interview an older person. You might be able to help with some of the research for a particular project and in the process pick up a few facts for yourself.

With younger children on outings you can play 'learning together' games where you might decide to count the number of steps you come to, or count how many yellow cars you can see or even use those old standbys such as 'I spy with my little eye, something that begins with…' and 'Guess what I'm thinking of in 21 questions, the first question being "Animal, vegetable or mineral"'.

'Animal, vegetable or mineral' is a game where children's imaginations come to the fore as they think of the most bizarre things to trap adults. One child I played this game with chose 'a piece of Captain Cook's poo' (obviously a seven-year-old boy) as the object to be guessed. The amazing thing is that some astute questions were able to lead to the correct answer, right on question 21.

...learning together games

Games like this can be great learning experiences. They help grandchildren and grandparents develop relationships, the child's mind is exercised and new things are learned. And, of course, they help to pass the time.

Remembering the details

You might be the sort of person who can remember everyone's name, all of the birthdays and exactly what all of the relations have done in the last five years. If you are, congratulations! If you're not, you're in the majority. You're also more likely to be a male.

With our declining memories, or perhaps with the threat that our memories may decline one day, we need a crib sheet, or at least a notebook or diary, or failing that, an extremely reliable partner who is able to remember everything.

Do you remember all the birthdays? Okay, you can? Well done. Do you remember the presents you gave last year so as not to do a repeat this year? Do you remember the names of their pets? 'Yes', you say to these last two. Okay, how about some harder ones. What are the names of their preschool teachers or their schoolteachers? What are the names of the teachers they had last year? What are their friends' names? See, it's getting a little harder.

When I was a boy I was always impressed by how well our family doctor remembered the details of our family. It wasn't that we were the family from hell that you just couldn't forget. He would remember things I was interested in and other family details which weren't particularly related to my current bout of tonsillitis or tummy ache.

Perhaps he had a prodigious memory, but I often wondered if he kept a few notes and brushed up on them before each consultation. I don't have a prodigious memory, so for many of my patients I kept a few notes on the inside cover of the patient folder. I'd jot down the names of the siblings whom I'd been told about, but usually hadn't ever seen, bits of information about school and interests and then have a quick look before the next consultation. Then I could say, 'How's Julie's netball going?' or 'Is Clive still having tuba lessons?' As I'd usually only be seeing these children every six or 12 months for a review, these memory feats would impress everyone. It wasn't that I did it just to pretend to be interested. I really was interested, but without the little memory prompts strategically placed on a corner of the notes I would have been floundering, probably asking Clive about netball and Julie about tuba lessons.

One way to stay on top of the memory game with grandchildren is to use a notebook. A small ring-bound one where you can insert pages and use colour dividers to separate each grandchild is good. Then you can list the obvious stuff like their mum's and dad's name (just in case you're having a horrendous memory day), their birthdays, favourite foods, friends' names, teachers' names, gifts given and received, and current likes and dislikes. You won't want to leave it lying around. After all, you want to give the impression that you hold all of these facts in your agile mind. If you're a computer-literate grandparent you might want to set up this information on your computer.

Then all you have to do is remember where you last left the notebook or the password you decided to use on the computer file.

GIFTS AND GIVING

The reaction and appreciation of your grandchildren to gifts will depend on their ages and their upbringing. Many one year olds seem to enjoy the paper the gift was wrapped in more than the gift itself. It's always fascinating to see the baby scrunch up and tear the paper, thoroughly immersed in the pleasure this gives and quite oblivious of the present the wrapping paper held...particularly if it was a pair of pyjamas or a hand-knitted beanie. In contrast, the sophisticated or over-indulged late teenager may need an all expenses paid holiday to Bali to create the same level of excitement.

Gifts should be safe

You don't want your grandchild to cut off his finger with the Swiss army knife you have just given him or to poke out his sister's eye with his new Star Wars light sabre. On the other hand, you don't want to give presents which are so deadly boring that there are family jokes, when you aren't around, about 'grandma's and grandpa's gifts'. It's good to discuss gifts with the parents in advance as they can advise what the child would really like and in doing so give approval for any particular gift.

Have you visited one of those mega-toy stores recently? The sheer number and variety of toys available can be overwhelming, compared with when we were young parents. You'll also remember from your own parenting experiences that toys aren't always used in the way they were meant to be, so when thinking of safety, consider all the possible ways that the toy could be used, or misused, including use by a younger brother or sister. A useful guide is to ask yourself, 'Is this a toy that I could stand having at my place?'

If it's one that emits loud screeches, bangs and beeping electronic sounds, it may not pass the test. 'So what?' you say. 'It will be at their house, not mine.' The parents might have their revenge, however, by sending the toy with the grandchild whenever he visits you, so that you too can share in the suffering...until you quietly remove the batteries.

Many fancy toys of this nature hold little interest for children after the first few minutes. The toys that really hold attention are the ones that can be incorporated into games and which stimulate the imagination. Toys that are miniature representations of life, or of imaginary life, are best: plastic figures, cars, dolls, animals (including dinosaurs for four- to six-year-old boys) and building blocks can be incorporated into a variety of games. In the course of this play your grandchildren will act out their experiences, use their imagination, develop their fine motor skills as they build things and will carry out experiments. They might even give you the ultimate compliment of asking you to join in. Don't take over, just sit on the floor with them and do what they tell you to do. Just mucking around is an important part of play and learning.

These are the sorts of toys your grandchildren will enjoy and their parents will thank you for. More elaborate toys, tempting though they may be, have a place but interest is quickly lost if they don't stimulate the imagination and allow creative play.

Of course, the gift has to be appropriate for the child's age. For older children, you might be able to think of gifts which will open up new areas of interest for them, such as a theatre ticket, a magazine subscription, a diary or a special notebook. If you buy a theatre or a concert ticket as a birthday gift, you might want to buy extra tickets and take them. That way you can have fun too. You don't have to wait until they are teenagers for this sort of thing. There are puppet shows, pantomimes and baby proms suitable for children from two or three years of age which can also be fun for young-minded grandparents.

Books

Have you looked in the children's section of a bookshop lately? You'll be captivated. The only problem will be deciding what book to choose. You can start buying books from the early months of your grandchild's life and then watch them graduate from the small board books that a baby can hold and which have a bright picture on each page, through to Harry Potter and everything in between. The combination of good artwork and a short, intriguing story, often with a little humour, is just the thing to develop a love of books in children. Sure, they'll all grow up to become computer whizzes, but developing a love for books in the early years can help lay down a lifelong interest.

It's one of the joys of grandparenting to have a child snuggle up next to you while you read a story, point out the pictures and answer their questions. They enjoy the rhythm of the language and the repetition, which is such an important part of children's books. In the process, they improve their vocabulary, have their imagination stimulated and get to know you better. As they grow older and start to read by themselves, they might enjoy reading you a story. Or at that stage you can try reading a story together, with you and your grandchild taking turns to read out loud the lines of one of the different characters. Later, as they start to read more widely, you might want to read some of the books they read so that you can talk about them together. The other nice thing for a grandparent who reads the same books as their grandchildren is that the print is usually a little bigger, which makes it easier for us.

Reading the same books as your grandchildren can continue right through high school. One friend read all of the prescribed books his teenagers were given at high school. At an age when adolescents, parents and grandparents have little in common, having a chat about the book you've all been reading can help bridge that gap. You also get to read some really good books.

The practical gift

Some gifts are practical, but not much fun. Do you get excited when someone gives you a pair of socks, a tea towel, a pack of handkerchiefs or a knitted toilet roll cover? It's hard for grandchildren to get excited over things like pyjamas and underwear unless they have a lurid picture of the child's latest fad, such as Bob the Builder or the Saddle Club, on them. That doesn't mean you shouldn't give practical presents. They are often appreciated by the parents, if not by the child. It just means that it's worth supplementing the practical present with something that may be inexpensive, but which will be fun for the child.

Timely gifts

It's probably not wise to develop a reputation for always appearing with a gift, particularly expensive gifts. After all, you want your grandchildren to love you for your sparkling wit and personality, your wisdom and your thoughtfulness, for who you are, not for what you give. On the other hand, you don't always have to wait for birthdays and Christmas, particularly if there is something your grandchild needs right now. If your grandson or grand-daughter needs a new soccer ball (yes, girls play soccer too these days) there's not much point in giving it for their September birthday, right at the end of the soccer season. Give it as a spontaneous, un-birthday present in March to be ready for the beginning of the season. Just check with the parents that they aren't planning to do the same thing.

Saying thank you

Were you brought up to say, 'thank you'? Did you bring your children up to say, 'thank you'? We all like to be thanked, even when we say we don't. What do you do if your grandchildren forget to say thank you? Or if you send them a gift in the mail and you don't ever hear that they received it. Perhaps it went astray in the postal system. You just don't know. It's a common complaint. There's not very much you can do. You might want to remind them, or remind their parents, to say thank you for that birthday gift, but it doesn't help to make it a big issue.

Perhaps they just didn't like it and haven't reached our stage of sophistication where we say thank you to things we don't want and don't like. Probably all you can do, apart from wondering whether you raised their parent correctly, is to be a good role model and make sure that you use 'thank you' appropriately when they give you a gift or do something for you.

Encouraging giving and generosity

It is true that it is 'more blessed to give than to receive'. Grandparents can have a special role in encouraging giving and generosity in their grandchildren. Depending on your circumstances, and after discussion with the parents, you may want to do something such a sponsoring a child in a developing country in your grandchild's name and helping your grandchild write to the child and perhaps even make a regular contribution from pocket money towards the sponsorship.

You might be able to help them develop an interest in the less privileged members of society through your own interest and practical involvement. If you are a volunteer in a community group or belong to a service organisation you may be able to let your grandchildren be involved in some of those activities providing you have their parent's permission and that the planned activity will be fun for your grandchild.

Deciding to give some money away is one thing. Making a choice about the best place to give it is another. One nice idea is to give your grandchild two equal amounts of money, say $50. One amount of $50 is for them to decide how to use for themselves—for example, bank it all; bank some of it; buy a few shares; put it towards that MP3 player they are saving for; buy something they really need; use it when they go on holidays or take the family to the movies with it. The other $50 is for them to give away. They can look into several charities that interest them, decide which they like best and then decide if they want to give it all to one charity or if they want to divide it amongst two or more charities and if so, in what proportion.

Instilling a concept of using some money wisely on themselves or their family and also using money wisely to help others is a valuable lesson. And in the unlikely event that your grandchild grows up to make it into the BRW Rich List, you may find that these early values you helped to form will have a significant impact on the community.

YOUR WILL

Did you know that almost 50 per cent of Australians die without having a valid will? It's probably because we find it hard to face the fact that one day we will no longer be here. Are you one of those without a will? If so, put this book down and phone your solicitor now. But just before you do, it's a good idea to decide what to put in your will. Most people keep it simple, leaving almost everything to their partner and children with some additional provision for favourite charities or causes.

Do you include your grandchildren in your will? That's up to you. You may want to make a provision for them, but remember if you do, have you allowed for any subsequent grandchildren who may arrive after your untimely demise and your estate (feeble, or otherwise) has been distributed.

These things are worth discussing with a solicitor. It's also good to let your family know the broad details of your will. It goes without saying that if you want to continue to be loved and respected as a grandparent, rather than feared, don't use being 'in the will' or 'out of the will' as a bribe or a threat.

WHEN THEY COME TO STAY

Long visits from grandchildren have two high points: when they arrive and when they leave. That's not an anti-grandchild statement, as grandparents will understand. It is fun having them, but it's also good to put the house back together again and recharge your energy stores after they leave.

As adults often have their children at a later age these days, it follows that many modern grandparents take on this role at a later age than their own grandparents did. Two generations ago, when young people often married in their early twenties or younger, it wasn't unusual to become a grandparent in your early forties. Now, with first children arriving when a couple may be in their mid-thirties, it's not unusual for some people to become grandparents for the first time in their late sixties or even seventies. And 60 year olds and 70 year olds don't have quite as much energy as 40 year olds.

Plan the visit in advance

If the grandchildren are coming to your place for a day, a weekend or a longer stay, it's worthwhile doing a little planning:

- Do your household jobs in advance. There won't be much spare time once the grandchildren arrive.
- Safety-proof the house (see Chapter 10, Giving Your Grandchild Back in One Piece).
- Work out in advance what you'll need to do should they become ill.
- Let them bring some of their own special toys, especially their favourite soft, cuddly toy which gives them security.
- Pull out from your storage area some of the toys their parents had when they were children. You couldn't bear to throw them away, could you? Now is your chance to recycle them and the grandchildren will love playing with them.

- Plan some activities in advance.
- Don't be disappointed if the grandchildren don't want to do what you have planned. You can't *make* children have fun. Just set up situations where the fun can happen.
- Have a wet weather plan.
- Be flexible.
- Tolerate a mess.

Most importantly, don't criticise their parents in front of them. You may not agree with their child-rearing techniques, their approach to discipline, the way they handle their money, or the informalities of their own relationship. ('Why on earth don't they get married?' you hear yourself say.) You may disapprove of some of their friends, or even of the partner your child has chosen. These are not views grandchildren should ever hear or even see by your gestures and behaviour.

Of course, you and your partner might want to have a quiet whinge about something your children have been doing, but this is for your private moments only—very private moments. Children are remarkably good at hearing things they are not supposed to hear, or picking up subtle disapproval in a sarcastic comment.

DISCIPLINE

This is a vexed question. What do you do if there are behaviour problems? Should you let them get away with anything and everything? Should you tell their parents?

Children like a framework, a structure and rules. They respond to this, especially from about five years of age, so you can capitalise on this. The golden rule is to stick to the rules the parents have made. You may be able to indulge them more when they visit, and you probably should, but the broad framework for rules and standards should still apply. You may agree to let them go to bed 30 minutes later than usual, but you don't let them stay up for an extra two hours to watch an M-rated video with you.

It's good for the basic rules to be clear at the start of the visit, such as no running out on the road, no hitting each other and all the other things which their parents have decreed and on which you and their parents need to be consistent, even if you don't totally agree with all of them.

They may be little angels for much of the time but they may also try to pull the wool over your eyes, such as, 'At home we don't have to clean our teeth', or 'Mummy and Daddy let us stay up till eleven o'clock on Friday night'. Don't be a pushover just to be popular. Grandparents have the delegated authority of the parents when they are minding their children. As long as the rules and boundaries are consistent and applied fairly, there can be some grandparently indulgence within these boundaries and you can all have fun

TRAPS TO AVOID

At the end of Chapter 2 there were some tips on things to avoid. Here are some further tips. Don't:

- tell them they can do something at your place that they're not allowed to do at home
- make a promise you can't keep
- lie to them
- swear in front of them or tell off-colour jokes. You're sure to be quoted again and again
- have favourites among the grandchildren
- ask grandchildren which set of grandparents they prefer
- criticise or belittle them
- threaten them (particularly with a threat you can't keep)
- smoke in front of them. It will shorten your life anyway so you may as well give up so as to enjoy your grandchildren for longer
- criticise their parents even when you think the children are out of earshot. Grandchildren have an amazing facility for hearing things not meant for their ears
- buy them a pet without first consulting their parents.

5

Outings with Grandchildren

You've planned this terrific outing with your three-year-old and five-year-old grandchildren. You found a lovely picnic area near a lookout, just a 20-minute drive away, followed by a short walk along a clearly marked bush track. The views are stunning and you're planning a picnic overlooking the valley. You've packed the grandchildren's favourite foods and a few toys, just in case they need distracting. You buckled them into the approved child restraints in the back seat and off you go, full of expectations.

As it turns out, there are several things you didn't allow for. The first was a burst water main on the main road, causing stop–start traffic so that the first half of the journey takes 75 minutes. Your two adorable grandchildren are pinching each other and the youngest, little Scott, is saying over and over, 'I do wee-wee. I do wee-wee'. You can't tell if he's already done it or if he just wants to do it. You can't stop, so you optimistically say, 'Hold on, dear'.

The traffic finally clears and you do the last 10 kilometres, which is along a winding road, at a good speed, trying to make up time. All those bends aren't good for young Prunella's stomach. You forget that her mother said that she tends to get carsick on winding roads. She throws up. Fortunately it misses your car's upholstery, but unhappily for young Scott, most of it lands on his head. Scott now smells of sour milk and Coco Pops at his top end and like a urinal at his bottom end.

You finally reach the car park. Scott skins his knees when he runs ahead on the bush track and falls over. Just as you lay out the picnic on the rock, the sky darkens, there is a tremendous crack of thunder, lightning scars the sky and torrential rain pelts down. Prunella slips on the wet rock and plunges into the valley below. You can't raise emergency services on your mobile phone because you forgot to recharge it. Grandpa has a heart attack and little Scott keeps saying, 'I want my mummy...'

This, of course, is fantasy. No children were damaged in the creation of this story. But it does raise a few principles for outings with grandchildren.

USEFUL TIPS FOR OUTINGS

You will remember what it was like organising outings with your own children. Here is a reminder of some useful tips for outings with your grandchildren.

Be flexible
Children, especially young children, have short attention spans, so plan outings that are short in duration and long on variety. Be prepared to change your plans and have an alternative plan in case of bad weather, traffic jams, illness or other unexpected events that could make your planned outing a disaster if you went ahead.

Be prepared
Take a bag or rucksack with some essentials: a change of underwear (for the children, not for you, unless you really need one); clean clothes; a fold-up umbrella if the weather looks suspicious; a plastic bag for the dirty stuff; wipes; tissues; spare nappies; change of clothes; sunscreen; some water and a variety of nutritious snacks.

Check out the venue first
If you're going to a park, on a bushwalk or a place you haven't been to before, it's worthwhile checking out the route first, the best way to get there, any potential hazards and the availability of facilities such as water and toilets.

It doesn't have to be extravagant

You don't have to spend a fortune. Simple outings can be just as much fun, sometimes more fun than extravaganzas.

Use outings as teaching opportunities

Use the outing as a good time to remind your grandchildren about road safety, watching for on-coming cars, using pedestrian crossings and learning how to cross at traffic lights.

Remember car safety

Your precious grandchildren can only travel in your car if you have suitable, approved car restraints for their age and size. Never leave them in the car alone, even for a moment, and don't give them the car keys to play with. They may just press the button and lock themselves and the keys inside. See Chapter 10 for more information on car safety with grandchildren.

Keep car journeys as short as possible

Remember when your children fought in the back seat and kept asking, 'Are we there yet?' Their children are likely to do it, too.

Try using public transport

If you live in an area where there is reasonable public transport, try it out. It can be great fun for grandchildren who may have had little or no experience of buses, trains and ferries. If you've reached the venerable age where you qualify for a senior's discount, it's cheap, too. In fact, you will find that you'll be paying more for your grandchildren than for your own ticket.

As your grandchildren become a little older, they'll enjoy reading the timetables, working out which train or bus to catch, getting the connections timed perfectly and working out which train platform to wait on.

You may even find your own children prefer you to use public transport. We may have been ace car drivers in our youth, and are probably still pretty good, but the time will come when our reflexes aren't quite as sharp, and our necks don't swivel as well and our sense of timing leaves a little to be desired. You may find your children subtly suggesting that they prefer you to use public transport, rather than drive their children about. Don't be offended, take the hint. It's more fun anyhow.

Be a good role model

Children think that their grandparents are wonderful. At least the younger ones do. Use outings as opportunities to teach them good values. Not just safety when crossing the road, but also courtesy, respect, tolerance and humour. Outings are a great opportunity to do this, not in a 'preaching' way, but just in conversation and by our own behaviour. Of course, it's essential not to undermine or criticise their parents or the things their parents do. Just set a good example.

Bring home as many as you took out

If you plan to go out with three grandchildren, make sure that you take all three when you leave. You don't want to arrive at the train station to find that you've left one behind in the house. Similarly, if you leave with three grandchildren, bring three home (try to make it the same three as you left with).

STRANGER DANGER

When we were children, our parents taught us not to talk to strangers and never to go anywhere with a stranger. They never told us why, but of course they were worried about abduction and sexual abuse. We taught our children the same lesson and now that our society is much more aware of the extent of sexual abuse, it's an important lesson for our grandchildren, too. We now know that only about one-quarter of sexual abuse is caused by strangers, with the majority of offences being perpetrated by people the child knows and trusts, including people in the child's family, even some grandparents. But as it's a common problem, we still need to be concerned about the 25 per cent or so of cases caused by strangers. We also know that the stereotype of the man loitering on the corner in a raincoat, tempting a child with candy, is far from true. Many abusers are charming and appear to be kind and helpful.

Prevention involves supervision and education. Many schools now have good Protective Behaviour programs which teach children about not letting people they don't know come closer than an arm's length and which also give advice about avoiding risky situations. Good as these programs may be, they are no substitute for parental (and grandparents') teaching and most importantly, supervision, particularly of younger children.

So what do you do when on an outing with the grandchildren? Before you leave home, remind them of the rules about not wandering away, not running off and not going with strangers. Be vigilant so that you can always see them. If you can, take the other grandparent. Two sets of eyes and hands help. A second grandparent can be particularly helpful when little Nathan needs to go to the toilet. Grandfather can take him to the gents while Grandma takes Amanda to the ladies. If there is only one grandparent and the inevitable, 'I want to do wee-wee' occurs, you can probably get away with taking young children of both sexes to the same toilet. Once they are about five or six years old, however, they are likely to object. You may then have to let them go in alone, telling them to be quick, to call you in a loud voice if they are worried while you stand close outside, hoping no-one wonders what you are doing loitering outside a public toilet.

One of my patients, a three-year-old girl, was abducted by a stranger who tempted her into the back of his panel van with a white rabbit which he let the little girl pat. The girl went into the van to see the rabbit and the man drove off with her. Fortunately, the alarm was raised very quickly, the van was sighted by the police within 30 minutes and the girl was rescued before any harm was done.

She seemed fine, but we used the opportunity to reinforce with her the importance of never going with a person she didn't know. Even though she was just three, we thought we'd got the message across fairly clearly until at the end of the discussion, the social worker said, 'So, Melanie, you'd never get into a car with a stranger again, would you?' Melanie thought for a moment, then her eyes lit up and she said, 'I would if he had a rabbit!' Teaching is important for young children, but it can't be totally relied upon. At this stage there is no substitute for constant vigilance.

OUTINGS WITH PRESCHOOLERS

Preschoolers are high in energy but often low in concentration, so outings are best kept short and simple. Like their grandparents, they don't function as well when they are tired and hungry. Also like their grandparents, they like a regular afternoon sleep, so allow for that. They tend to throw up when they are upset and don't mind announcing their toilet needs in a loud and urgent voice, wherever they may be. They may wander off, so keeping them always in sight is important.

For this age group the emergency pack of spare clothes, nappies, wipes, snacks and drinks is essential. They burn up lots of energy and quickly become hungry and thirsty. A small container holding slices of cheese and cracker biscuits, or whatever else is their current fad, can be invaluable. Another container holding cut-up fresh fruit or dried fruit helps too. Water is the best drink to take on outings. They may want those small, boxed fruit drinks as well, which is fine, but a couple of bottles of water never goes astray. You can also use some of the water for cleaning them up.

As we saw in Chapter 3, this age group likes ritual, so don't be surprised if the next day they want to visit the same place, play the same games and eat the same food. They may even ask for a repeat of the previous outing on their next visit.

It takes time to get ready. If both grandparents are going on the outing this helps in terms of getting the children ready and supervising them on the outing. It will probably take longer than you think to get them ready, particularly if little Giselle insists on wearing her tutu and if three-year-old Carl, going through his Batman phase, insists on wearing his underpants on top of his jeans. To avoid the outing starting in tears and tantrums it's probably better to let Giselle wear her tutu and allow Carl to have his underpants on the outside if that's what he wants. They may attract a few stares and comments, but you can get away with a lot when you're young and cute. And you can always say, 'Oh, we're just minding them for someone'.

Visits to the park

Preschoolers love parks with slides, swings and climbing frames. It's worth checking out the park first for safety features. Some children's parks are fenced with a self-latching gate which means that you can let them run around more freely, knowing that they can't escape.

Walks

The walk can be a really exciting activity, particularly if you can walk to something interesting: a construction site where tractors or graders are at work; the shops where they can have a milkshake, ice cream or a baby-cino, or a lake or river...so long as you hold their hands.

As well as using a walk to reinforce pedestrian traffic rules, you can talk with them and play games such as seeing how many flowers, leaves, birds, yellow cars, buses, lizards, red-bellied black snakes, dung beetles or dinosaurs they can spot. They may like to play simple games such as jumping on all of the cracks, avoiding the cracks, or walking backwards at times.

After rain it's fun to put on old clothes and appropriate shoes and go for a walk where they can try to jump in every puddle along the path. Then head back home to a warm bath and a hearty snack.

You'll need to be prepared for the request, 'I want to be carried' on outings, so it's worthwhile having a fold-up stroller that the younger ones may be able to use at times.

Bushwalks

If you can easily get to a safe bush track, this makes an ideal walk for three- to five-year-olds and you can all let your imagination run riot as you pretend to explore the area, hunt for treasure, look up for fairy bowers and avoid man-eating wild animals.

Trains, buses and ferries

Try using two different types of transport to add interest to the trip, and end up somewhere where you can share a treat with them, such as a visit to a children's bookstore, a gelato bar or even fish and chips if their parents approve.

...look but don't buy

Pet shops

A trip to a pet shop is good for preschoolers, and most pet shop owners seem reasonably tolerant. If you want to remain on good terms with mum and dad, just make sure before you go that the grandchildren know the visit is to look and not buy.

Swimming pools

Visits around water are more easily done with two grandparents. Many pools have excellent paddling areas for toddlers. They will use up lots of energy and be very hungry, and hopefully sleepy, afterwards.

Ball pits and adventure play areas

Some shopping malls have adventure play areas and ball pits where toddlers and preschool-aged children can crawl through a maze of tunnels, ladders and platforms and tumble around on coloured polystyrene balls. Some are even set up so that grandparents can sit with a cup of coffee while keeping an eye on their charges. When grandpa has to crawl through the maze to rescue little Tamara, who has just been reduced to tears by the current adventure playground bully, it's not quite as dignified and relaxing.

Freebies and almost freebies

Some museums, such as those for natural history or technology are free to children under the age of four and occasionally free, or at least very inexpensive, for seniors. Don't expect to cover the whole museum. The preschooler will only want to spend time at a few exhibits, generally the ones set up to let children touch and do things.

More elaborate outings

Zoos, aquariums and nature parks are always popular. Just remember that there will be a fair bit of walking, time will be needed for rests and snacks and that preschoolers will probably only have the energy and interest to see some of the animals. That leaves plenty to see on the next visit.

OUTINGS WITH FIVE TO TEN YEAR OLDS

Your grandchildren are now at school. They know a lot. In fact, some know everything. They are starting to develop interests of their own and may appreciate being able to choose which outing they would like, from an option of two or three. Many of the outings suggested for preschoolers are also good for this age group if done at a more sophisticated level.

Puppet shows

If a touring puppet show is in the area, make the most of it. Grandparents enjoy them, too.

Pantomimes

Amateur theatre groups sometimes put these on during holiday periods. They involve lots of action, movement and singing as well as audience participation.

Follow a treasure map

A variation on the walk is to draw up a map of local streets that they can follow with you to find that the treasure map leads you all to an ice-cream shop or some other venue that will appeal to them.

A visit to the shopping mall

Malls often put on shows for children during school holidays such as singing groups, dancers, puppet shows and even magicians. One of the hazards of the modern shopping mall is the food court with its numerous fast-food outlets. It's good to decide with the grandchildren (and their parents) in advance whether or not you will eat there for a treat and, if so, what the limits are. Alternatively, you can always avoid the food court and take your own healthy snacks.

Libraries

A visit to the children's section of a local library can help foster an interest in books and reading. Many libraries have readings for children at regular times. Your local council will be able to provide you with information of events.

Aquariums, zoos and wildlife parks

They are good for this age group as well as for preschoolers. At this age, they'll probably want to see everything and you'll be the one who is worn out first.

Fishing

If you love untangling fishing lines, this is for you. Sitting on the edge of a wharf, hanging onto a grandchild with one hand, helping to bait his hook, untangling his line and finding, as you pull it in, that the thing tugging on the end of it is a mud crab with a pincer the size of your forearm is an experience that is hard to beat. Keep calm, so that amidst the ensuing chaos, you aren't in the situation where your grandchild topples off the edge of the wharf, leaving you to face the advancing crab alone.

A good rule of thumb is to have as many adults as children on a fishing trip—that is, two grandchildren need two adults. Some states have regulations about fishing licences, even for recreational fishing, so check this first.

OUTINGS WITH ELEVEN YEAR OLDS AND OLDER

Pre-teenagers and young teenagers want to feel grown up, so involve them in the plans for the outing. They may also be much happier if they can bring a friend. At this age, we are no longer the centre of their interests. We may just be a means of them getting on the outing, something we may remember from our own children although, if we've developed good relationships with them as they've been growing up, they may still enjoy our company. But don't expect them to prefer us over their friends.

By the time they get to this age we'll be ten or more years older than when they were toddlers, so thankfully we don't have to run after them as often. And if we did, we wouldn't be able to catch them anyway. Here are some suggestions for outings for older grandchildren.

Concerts
They may choose a different one from the type you'd prefer, but this is also the opportunity to introduce them to different kinds of music.

Movies
You'll probably find that the obligatory popcorn and drink will cost almost as much as the ticket. Choose movies that have their parents' approval and that are rated G (general viewing) or perhaps PG (parental guidance). Movies rated M and MA15+ are for mature viewers, not for your young grandchildren.

Sporting events
You might find that your own children want to be in on this outing too, particularly if you have been able to secure tickets that are hard to get.

The theatre

Choose a play that will be suitable for them. It may be the beginning of a lifelong interest in theatre and if so, an opportunity for future outings and for giving theatre tickets as birthday and Christmas presents.

Ice skating

This works well if they bring a friend, rather than expect you to skate with them. Old bones break more easily.

Shopping

As long as it's to buy stuff for them and not for you, a shopping outing can be very appealing to this age group. A good idea is to set the ground rules in advance about how much money will be spent.

Something special

For youngsters growing up, an eating adventure with grandparents can be something special that they may not normally do with their own parents. If it's within your budget, dress up and have lunch at a smart hotel or restaurant or arrange an outing for a special afternoon tea at a hotel.

If you can afford to do something special every now and then, do it, but don't do it too often, to ensure that it remains special. Part of a child's development involves learning that they can't have everything they want, that there will always be children who have more than they have and perhaps grandparents who do more and give more than their grandparents. It also involves understanding that having expensive things and going on exotic outings doesn't correlate particularly well with being happier. As grandparents, we can help our grandchildren to understand these concepts by doing things which bring happiness without being constantly over-indulgent.

6

Some Special Situations

Families are diverse. They vary in composition, backgrounds, behaviours and beliefs. They aren't all composed of two Caucasian parents and two well-mannered children standing behind a white picket fence, contrary to what we've been led to believe at times. And they don't all have two sets of benign grandparents with grey hair, twinkling eyes, the ability to make the best apple pies and tell the best yarns...although some do have grandfathers who are good cooks and grandmothers who talk a lot.

Families also consist of single parents, divorced parents, remarried parents, step-children and grandparents who may have been single, divorced or remarried. Parents die. Children die. Some families have members with disabilities, some have domestic violence, alcohol and drug abuse. Some have a parent in prison. Some families have single sex parents, some consist of mixed racial groups, some have blends of different religions and many have no religion at all. As one of the few certainties of life is death, let's start off looking at death: the death of a parent, death of a grandchild and death of a grandparent.

DEATH

Death, like weddings and christenings, can be a time when questions of belief and faith may resurface and when for some families the observance of specified ceremonies related to the funeral, the burial and the period of mourning may be particularly important. It is a time when tensions may arise if there are strongly held differences of opinion in the family or if the family is a mixture of different cultures. Some cultures and religious practices have strict rules about the type of burial or the time allowed to lapse between the death and the burial. Some don't approve of cremation; some grieve silently; others grieve in a much more vocal and open way. Some like to spend time with the deceased person, while others don't. Many of these customs have evolved over the centuries. They have been found to be helpful in coping with the loss, in understanding the finality of death or in looking to a future life. Grandchildren may ask questions about these things. Honest answers will help them in their grieving and in their understanding of the diversity of beliefs and cultural practices in our society.

When a parent dies

The loss of a parent is hard to come to terms with at any age. If your grandchild loses a parent you will be dealing with your own grief and trying to support the grieving, surviving partner, a parent who has been thrown into a new role, that of a single parent. Your grandparenting role will also involve trying to understand and support your grandchildren who have lost part of the focus of their lives.

The most painful loss a child can experience is the loss of a parent they have loved and who has loved them. The child's life is changed forever. It's a time of confusion and sadness for the child as well as for the surviving parent.

We know that death is inevitable, universal and the end of our physical lives. What we don't know is when it will occur. Children's understanding of death is different and develops gradually.

Children under five don't have a strong sense of time, so 'final' and 'forever' are not well understood. They might think that death is a temporary state, like someone who goes away and then returns. They might ask, 'Why doesn't Mummy come back?'

Children between five and eight are starting to understand that death is final. If they've been exposed to movies and television where death is depicted, they might think of death as a result of violence or aggression. They're quite interested in the rituals surrounding death and should be involved in them, such as going to the funeral, if they wish. They may feel responsible: 'She got sick because I was naughty. I killed her.' This is a very good reason for not saying stupid things to children which suggest that their behaviour might kill you. You may just happen to die and they'll think they know why.

From nine years onwards, most children have an adult view of death. The best way to know what children think and feel about death is to listen to them.

It used to be thought that children didn't grieve. We now know that they do and that they experience similar feelings to those of bereaved adults. Children learn about loss from the earliest years. It may be when their mother decides to stop breastfeeding and that soft, warm feeling against their cheek, coupled with the sound of their mother's heartbeat, suddenly goes. They lose favourite toys, move house, lose friends, perhaps have a pet die. These losses may cause anger, confusion and sadness, feelings that will reappear far more intensely if they lose a parent. The way they cope with this loss will depend partly on their underlying personalities and also on how they are guided through the process.

Babies may react to the way those around them react. A grieving mother may have less emotional energy to give her child for a period and the child may respond by becoming sad and withdrawn. Primary school children may feel shock, anger and guilt, just as adults do. They may not show their feelings openly, so that adults may not realise how much they are affected. They may show a variety of behavioural changes, including aggression, bed-wetting, telling lies or becoming withdrawn.

What can grandparents do?

As well as coping with our own grief, we need to be supportive, understand why our grandchildren may be behaving differently and be honest and open in our communication with them. Answer their questions honestly, but don't overload them with information. Simple, factual terms such as 'dead' and 'has died' avoid confusion. Phrases such as 'passed away' and 'taken from us' don't make sense to children and can be misleading. Don't be afraid to cry. It's okay to show the child how much their parent meant to you as well.

Your grandchildren may have questions about death which they ask you. They may ask about heaven: 'Where is it?', 'Where is Mummy?', 'Will I meet her one day?', 'My friend at school says there is no such thing as heaven.' These are the questions which have exercised the minds of children, religious thinkers and philosophers for thousands of years. And now you have to answer them. A good way to respond is to find out what your grandchild has already been told as this may have led to their question. Then, answer as honestly as you can in a way that respects the beliefs of their parents and affirms any sincerely held beliefs you may have. Remember, too, that young children often don't want detailed explanations, just as much information as they can manage at that time. If they want to know more, they'l ask.

When a grandparent dies

It's the natural order of things for grandparents to die before their children and their grandchildren. At least we know, by the time we get to grandparent age, that death is somewhere on the horizon, hopefully the far horizon. The surviving grandparent has her (yes, women live longer, so statistically it will be a 'her') own grief to deal with.

It's a sobering thought that widowhood is the inevitable conclusion to all marriages or partnerships that don't end in divorce or separation. We lose the person on whom we've relied for physical and emotional companionship. We cease to be a wife or husband and become a widow or a widower. We have to adjust to loneliness, we may feel depressed, even suicidal, and may feel overwhelmed by the future as well as having no interest in it.

For most people it takes about a year to move through the stages of grief. During this time there will be a variety of reactions. There may be physical symptoms: fatigue, breathlessness, tightness in the throat and a dry mouth. Feelings may include anger, guilt, anxiety, loneliness, yearning, helplessness, sadness and self-reproach.

There may also be behavioural changes, which can include inability to sleep, poor appetite, dreams about your partner, crying, social withdrawal, and visiting places or treasuring objects that bring back memories. Thoughts can include disbelief, confusion, suicidal wishes and auditory and visual hallucinations.

Dr Elisabeth Kübler-Ross has described five stages of grief:

1. Denial: An initial denial that the loss has taken place. This may last only a few moments or, at times, much longer.
2. Anger: Anger at the world, at God, about the medical care and the hospital, at the deceased person for leaving them and at themselves for allowing the death to happen, even though they know inside that they could have done nothing to prevent it.
3. Bargaining: Some go through a process of bargaining, making bargains with God, such as 'If I do this, will you take away my loss?'
4. Depression: This may be accompanied by feelings of numbness and withdrawal, although anger and sadness may remain underneath.
5. Acceptance: A time comes when the anger, sadness and mourning taper off and the reality of the loss becomes accepted.

In the midst of all this, the surviving grandparent has a grandchild who has lost a grandparent. There may be quite intense grieving by the child if she was very close to the grandparent or if the grandparent played a parenting role in the grandchild's life. At other times, in our mobile and sometimes fractured society, the grandchildren may have rarely seen or had contact with their grandparents.

The basic rules are the same as for the child who has lost a parent: accept and respect the child's sadness, understand why there may be behaviour difficulties, answer questions honestly and simply without information overload, allow the grandchildren to attend the funeral if they wish, and don't be afraid to let them see your own grief.

When a grandchild dies

Around one baby in 100 is stillborn or dies in the first 28 days after birth. Most stillborn babies die before labour commences. Babies who die after birth usually do so from complications of extreme prematurity or a congenital abnormality which prevents them from adjusting to life after birth.

Grandparents become excited when their child is going to have a baby and have great expectations for that baby. Then the baby is stillborn or dies within a few days or weeks. They won't have had the chance to get to know the baby, but the grief is still there.

For the parents, particularly the mother who has carried the baby, the grief is intense. This grief needs to be recognised by the grandparents. Don't suggest they 'forget about' the baby and start making another one. You may not be as crass as that, but you do need to avoid so-called comforting phrases such as, 'you can have another baby' or 'at least you still have your other children', and clichés like, 'you're young, you'll get over it', 'time will heal' and 'at least it wasn't older', a doubly offensive phrase, referring to the baby as 'it'. Respect their feelings, talk about the baby with them and use the baby's name. This will help your grieving process, too.

The parents will most likely give their stillborn child a name. It's good to hold a funeral, recognising that this baby has been part of the family and will remain part of the family in memory and in subsequent conversations.

Sarah and Tim were expecting their first child. Everyone was looking forward to the event. Sarah had been fit and well throughout the pregnancy. The only change she noted, apart from the obvious physical ones, was that from the moment she became pregnant she disliked the smell of freshly brewed coffee. Then, two weeks before the date of delivery, Sarah suddenly noticed that freshly brewed coffee smelt good again. And she noticed that the baby had stopped kicking. An urgent ultrasound showed that there was no heartbeat. The baby had died. Labour had to be induced. It was long, difficult and sad.

Sarah and Tim named their little girl Joy. They held Joy, talked to her and held each other. Other family members visited the labour ward and met Joy, too. The hospital staff were caring and sensitive. Tim arranged the funeral, conducted by their minister friend who had married them, and Tim, accompanied by Sarah, carried the tiny white coffin himself. Lots of family and many friends came. It was a time of sadness but also a time of renewal of friendships and strengthening of family relationships. I know. My wife and I were there. Joy was our grand-daughter.

A miscarriage is also a loss that needs to be recognised. In particular, the mother's need to grieve shouldn't be glossed over. As termination of pregnancy is common in our society we may forget that the loss of a very much wanted baby, even though very early in pregnancy, is a real loss which brings with it many of the emotions that the loss of a child involves.

The normal grieving process has to take place and grandparents, who will be grieving themselves, can be supportive both emotionally and practically. The passage of time helps, but the emotion will always be there. Dr Sheila Kitzinger's words sum it up: 'Gradually, the space between the pain will get longer and the death of a baby becomes woven as one vivid strand in the whole texture of life.'

Death of an older grandchild

Children aren't supposed to die. When a grandchild dies, the grief of the grandparents is complicated. They mourn for a grandchild whom they have grown to love and they also feel helpless because they can't take away the pain felt by their own child, the parent.

Grandparents may go through the five stages of grief described by Dr Kübler-Ross, but grandmothers and grandfathers may grieve a little differently from each other. Women tend to find it easier to talk to others about their feelings and so may have more support than men. Sometimes men, particularly grandfathers, because they are of that generation before the Sensitive New Age Guy was invented, tend to 'act strong' and may not reveal their true emotions, feeling it's weak to show their vulnerability. They may keep busy and avoid talking about the death. This is their way of coping and it should be respected. Although a former Australian politician famously said, 'Balmain boys don't cry', it's okay for grandfathers to shed some tears.

Sometimes grandparents who outlive a grandchild worry that the death seems against the natural order. They may feel guilty, wondering why they couldn't have died instead.

Grandparents often receive little support. There aren't many books or support groups for grieving grandparents. They are usually left to cope as best they can. You may need to find support from your family doctor, a Community Health Centre, a church organisation, family and friends (although, at times, well-meaning advice from friends can be very irritating), or from reading. There isn't much written for grieving grandparents, but you may find it helpful to use a book on parental grieving and just substitute the word 'grandparent' for 'parent' as you read. This will also help you to understand your child's grief so that you can be more supportive.

Family get-togethers, birthdays and the anniversary of your grandchild's death may be stressful times and occasions when your children will appreciate your support. Be available to help out, particularly during the first year of grieving, to be supportive to the father as well as the mother, to listen, to talk about the child and the child's special qualities. Use the dead child's name in these conversations. Be ready to share memories and don't avoid opportunities for these conversations, staying alert to avoid the trite, unhelpful comments such as, 'be brave' and 'you must be strong for the other children'.

To be able to have loved someone and to have shared in their life is a privilege beyond price. Grief is the price we pay for loving.

DIVORCE

A hundred years ago death in young adult life was much more common. Women often died during childbirth. People died from infections which are now easily cured by a trip to the GP and a course of antibiotics. Widows and widowers often remarried. Divorce was rare. These days, the death of a young parent is much less common, but the divorce rate is high.

Divorce rates soared in Australia after the introduction of the no-fault Family Law Act in 1975 and private detectives, who had made a living bursting in on illicit liaisons with a flash camera, started to go out of business. In the 1950s, in Australia, a divorce, and the voyeuristic details, which were often required to achieve it, made juicy copy for evening newspapers.

Divorce usually involves children. Half (49.8 per cent to be precise) of the divorces in Australia in 2004 involved children, with more than 60 per cent of those children being younger than ten years old. The median age for divorce for men is 43 and 40 for women. The marriage has lasted an average of just under nine years and although divorce is far easier than it used to be, it still takes on average three and half years to complete all the paperwork and finalise financial matters.

Where do grandparents fit?

You'll most likely have mixed emotions about your child's divorce. If the marriage wasn't going well there may be some sense of relief. You'll be forced to look at your own beliefs and principles. Many of us in our fifties and sixties were brought up in a time when divorce was a rare event with considerable stigma. These views and principles may have governed our own relationships.

Although you probably had nothing to do with the events leading up to the divorce (if you did, you're in big trouble), you will feel a mixture of grief, discomfort and perhaps embarrassment. Your son or daughter may not have told you about their marital problems, perhaps because of embarrassment, but more likely because they feel it's their problem, not yours, and as independent adults they need to try to resolve it. You may feel that the sense of closeness you once had is not as strong and it may be the first time that you realise they are truly independent. In some situations the adults don't even tell their parents about the divorce, not for some time anyway. When one of their parents calls they may just say 'she's out' or 'he's away this weekend'. You'll have views and an opinion, which you may or may not keep to yourself, but it's worth remembering that you may only know one part of the story, mostly from one partner's perspective.

You may have strong negative feelings about the former partner, or you may have been quite close to them. This can raise problems if you still want to stay in touch with them and if you want to see your grandchildren when the former partner has access, as well as when your own child has them. You just need to be honest, not necessarily brutally honest, but let both parties know that you want to keep in touch, especially when the grandchildren are there. If you try to do it by stealth and deception, you'll come a cropper and this is when relationships will become really difficult.

Don't show favouritism to the former partner. Family loyalty is important too, even if you are angry with your own child for letting the situation occur. You still need to be supportive. Your child may find a new partner whom you may like or dislike. That new partner may already have children and so you suddenly become an instant step-grandparent. You'll be fairly busy working on enhancing those new relationships while still finding time to be there for your original grandchildren.

What about the grandchildren?

It will be a confusing time for them. They may feel responsible. They won't understand the reason for the divorce and may develop behaviour problems or become withdrawn. They will need stability and unconditional love. Their parents will still try to provide this, but they'll have plenty of other things on their minds.

Grandparents can provide extra support for the grandchildren. Be prepared to listen to them, accept them, love them and reassure them. You might be able to help out in practical ways with some extra babysitting, taking them to school or picking them up some of the time, doing all this while trying to cope with your own feelings about the situation.

What's really important is not to take sides in front of the grandchildren. Actually, it's smart not to take sides at all. You'll have opinions, but don't burden your grandchildren with them. It doesn't help. They have enough to cope with without being burdened by their grandparent's view. The grandparent's job is to listen, accept, provide practical help and be a point of security and stability in the child's world where the security and stability they have been used to suddenly seems precarious.

Of course for some children the separation of their parents may be a relief if there has been domestic violence and family chaos. Their new situation may bring increased security and stability, but they will still need that unconditional love and security which grandparents can provide and hopefully have been providing during the turbulent period leading up to the separation. They'll be comforted if you focus on them, let them know that you'll always be there for them and that you won't ever let them down.

Will I still see them?

This will depend partly on how well you have been getting on with the parents and also whether your own child in this situation is the mother or the father. As children usually live with their mothers after divorce, maternal grandparents find it easier to maintain relationships with their grandchildren. If the father doesn't have custody, or has little contact with the children, there is likely to be less contact with the paternal grandparents.

Some grandparents may apply for access through the Family Court, which is able to order grandparent access if the court decides this is in the best interests of the grandchildren. However, it is best to try to work out informal contacts; another reason for grandparents not to become involved in taking sides. The price may be that you don't get to see your grandchildren.

If you want to see your grandchildren:

- don't become involved in the dispute between your own child and the other parent
- be supportive of both parents

...not to take sides

- respect the role of the other parent. Don't undermine or denigrate them. You'll have your own view, of course, but keep it yourself or share it only with your partner. Never criticise the other parent in front of the grandchildren
- be flexible in the times you can spend with your grandchildren. Do this in a helpful way, such as offering to babysit, rather than demanding time.

A new set of grandchildren

Your child remarries or finds a new partner. This may be hard for your grandchildren to accept, particularly if they are young adults themselves and the new partner is as young as they are. They'll still feel loyalty to the other parent. Grandparents once again have a role in being supportive and listening, without being judgmental.

Or the new partner may already have children, so you suddenly have a few grandchildren that you hadn't expected, hadn't watched grow up and develop and don't know very well. What's your role here?

The step-grandchildren may also have a view about their new grandparents. This wasn't something they were seeking either. They've got enough coping to do with their new brothers and sisters. They will already have grandparents, so you may be superfluous, initially at least.

It will take time to get to know the new grandchildren. The relationship won't be the same as with your own grandchildren and it's unrealistic to expect that it will be and to expect that you'll feel the same love as for your own grandchildren. It's more realistic to work on building a relationship with them that is based on friendship.

When grandparents divorce

Grandchildren see their grandparents as constant and unchanging, so it can be confusing if their grandparents divorce or separate, or if they get a new boyfriend or girlfriend. They may wonder which one is the 'good' grandparent and which is the 'bad' one. The principles are similar to when parents divorce. There will be the dangers of asking the grandchildren to take sides, undermining the other partner in the separation and possibly giving in to anger, accusations and grief, emotions which grandparents aren't immune from either.

You will also need to reassure your grandchildren that your relationship with them is just as important as ever. Don't burden them with your troubles. If you are the grandparent who has been left, it's not realistic to expect your family to take you in and provide a life for you. They have their own lives to manage.

If you are going to separate, try to agree on what you'll tell your grandchildren (and what you won't tell them) and work out how you can both continue your roles as caring, supportive grandparents, focusing on the grandchildren's needs when you are with them rather than on your own. If you meet someone, you'll also have to think about how to introduce your new partner to the grandchildren. It's a bit like having new step-children. A good relationship between the new partner and the grandchildren will take time to establish, needn't be rushed and is best developed as a friendship.

OTHER FAMILY PROBLEMS

There can be a whole range of other family problems. Domestic violence, problems with alcohol and drugs and child abuse are among the most common.

Domestic violence

It is only in recent years that domestic violence has become recognised as a major problem in Australia. It's always been there, but it just wasn't talked about. Even now, according to an Australian Bureau of Statistics survey in 2005, only 36 per cent of women who experienced physical assault by a male partner reported it to the police. That's very concerning but it's an improvement on the situation ten years earlier, when only 15 per cent of cases were reported. That same survey found that 6 per cent of Australian women experienced domestic violence in the preceding twelve months. Men also experience domestic violence, the incidence being around 2 per cent.

If domestic violence is occurring in your child's family there is a good chance that your grandchildren will see it. Around 40 per cent of domestic violence is witnessed by children. Obviously this isn't good for them. Children who witness domestic violence may become aggressive, bully other children, deteriorate in their school performance and develop a range of behaviour problems, including running away from home.

What can you do if you think or know that domestic violence is occurring in your grandchildren's family? It's difficult. We're not supposed to interfere in our children's families. We can still be supportive, particularly of the grandchildren. They may want to spend more time with us. They may want to tell us things that we'd rather not hear.

You can obtain advice about how to help by calling the domestic violence hotline in your state. The hotlines are listed in the Appendix. If you can encourage your child or their partner, depending on who is the perpetrator, to make the complaint themselves, that's very worthwhile doing. Domestic violence won't go away. It's not a passing phase and its effects will damage your grandchildren. It's one of those occasions where some gentle advice, as well as unconditional support won't go astray.

If the situation is serious, and escalating, and if you are sure of the facts, it may be time to stop pussy-footing around and act. Call the domestic violence hotline and tell them what is happening and if their advice is to act—for example, by calling the police—then don't procrastinate, just do it.

Drugs and alcohol

These two problems are common in Australia and have similar effects on grandchildren as domestic violence. They may even occur as part of a set of family problems which include domestic violence. The grandparent's role is similar to that in domestic violence. Support the grandchildren as well as your own children. Use helplines for advice and encourage the parents to seek professional support. These things aren't passing phases and early, rather than late, intervention and support are essential.

Child abuse

There was a time when we thought child abuse was rare. It's only in the last 30 years that we've learned how common and widespread it is. Child abuse can include physical abuse, emotional abuse, neglect and sexual abuse. It's always been there, but the taboos on talking about it and even accepting that it occurs in nice, respectable families were very strong. We know now that it occurs right across the social spectrum, even in 'the best of families'.

Your grandchild may confide in you about abuse. If you're told something like this, you have a responsibility to do something about it. It's quite rare for children to make up stories of abuse, even though there is still a widespread view in the general public that they do.

It's not your job to hush it up or to go into hysterics or to play the detective or social worker to try to find out more. You can raise your concerns with the parents, or just with one parent if the child has told you about parental abuse, and encourage them to seek professional help. Child abuse is a crime and must not be covered up. Professionals need to become involved and the relevant authorities informed so that the child can be protected.

DIFFERENT FAMILY STRUCTURES

There seems to be a much wider range of family structures than when we were young parents. There are more single-parent families, more marriages between people of different ethnic and cultural backgrounds and more blended families as a result of divorce and remarriage.

Single-parent families

In Australia there are about a million children growing up in sole-parent families. This figure represents one-fifth of all Australian families. It follows that there will be many grandparents whose grandchildren live in a single-parent family. This may provide an extra role for the grandparent. The sole parent may need help with child care, financial assistance and just the ordinary emotional support that good parents give their children, whatever age their children may be. They will appreciate help, acceptance, and not criticism.

Your grandchildren may also need extra support. If they are living with their mother, they may appreciate extra time with their grandfather who, for the boy grandchildren, may become one of their male role models. The demands on your time for child care might be considerable, so you'll have to agree on some principles about how much time you'll be able to give. Realistic expectations by parents and grandparents alike will help.

A potential trap is to lavish too much care and attention on the single-parent family to the detriment of relations with your other children and grandchildren. The others may understand the need for this particular family to have some extra time, but they also want some of your attention. It's a balancing act for grandparents, but an important one if you want to avoid members of the family from feeling that you are neglecting them.

Blended families

This is really a new term for step-families. So many fairy stories in our generation told of wicked step-mothers or ugly step-sisters that it's not surprising someone thought up a new term. I suspect that most of these fairy stories were written by men, as there isn't much talk of wicked step-fathers or ugly step-brothers.

Blended families are common. Thirty-one per cent of men now marrying have children from a previous marriage. For women the figure is 33 per cent. The parents may still be sorting out their relationships from their previous partnership and may also have to work on developing relationships with the new family, including some new grandparents. We grandparents have to have realistic expectations. It's not realistic to expect that all the children will instantly get on well with each other.

Fortunately, the situation rarely turns out like Cinderella (virtual slavery) or Snow White (a murder plot involving poisoning) and we can work on developing friendships with the new children as well as with the new partner, even though we may have ambivalent feelings at times. The step-children will know they are different without their grandparents reminding them. The key to success is equal, equal, equal. Even if you're having difficulty in accepting the new partner, you have to mentally separate the child from the parent. There can be no differences in how you treat your grandchildren in quality and number of gifts, in attention and in behaviour. There is no place for favouritism—not ever.

Mixed marriages

We often talk about Australia being a successful multicultural country and most of the time it is. This means that, inevitably, there will be inter-marriage with a mixture of cultures, beliefs and religions.

If you are old enough to remember Australia under the White Australia Policy, you'll recall what a bland, boring place it could be. You might even have some old prejudices, or at least preconceived views left over from that era. If so, don't bring them to the relationship with your grandchildren. You'll be enriched by what you learn from being part of an inter-racial family.

Adoption

With many women deciding to have their children at a later age, their chance of conception decreases. Modern techniques, such as IVF, often come to the rescue, but not always. So your child and partner may decide to adopt a child. It's not as easy as it used to be as there aren't as many babies available for adoption. They may decide to adopt from overseas or, if they want to adopt in Australia, may be asked to consider adopting a child with a disability.

Wherever this new grandchild comes from, you will grow to love him even though he may not look very much like your own child. Development is an interplay between genetic factors and the environment. He'll develop similar tastes, interests and mannerisms to other family members and be just part of the family, even though he won't share their genes. He may show talents in areas that have never been seen before in your family, a result of his genetic features coming to the fore.

It's smart not to talk about 'real parents' and 'natural family'. That's confusing and could imply that the family raising him isn't natural. The biological family can be referred to as the birth family. His 'real' family will be the parents who have raised and nurtured him, although the time will come when he'll probably want to exercise his right to meet his birth parents.

It is extremely important that parents who adopt children tell them that they have been adopted and tell them this regularly from a very early age. The ideal is for adopted children to never be able to remember the day they were 'told they were adopted', because it was a concept they just grew up with from the earliest years. Most modern parents do tell their children, although there was much more reluctance to do so a generation or so ago.

Sometimes, if adopted children haven't been told but suspect that they were adopted, or if there are other situations such as illegitimacy, which the child comes to suspect, they may approach one of their grandparents for information. What do you do? Don't spill the beans. This is something between the child and the parents. You could suggest that your grandchild asks their parents and then you could warn the parents that the discussion is imminent.

One of the most important things about conversations such as this is that they should occur as good times, when the family is calm and rational, rather than have them come out during a crisis when feelings are high and tact and sensitivity are nowhere to be seen.

Grandparents, parents and grandchildren living together

This was the norm in the old days of the extended family and is still common in some cultures. There are advantages for the family in terms of learning, sharing, providing help for the parents, passing on experience and having more time with the grandchildren. There can also be problems such as lack of space when a grandparent and grandchild may have to share a bedroom, and grandparents interfering in trying to take over the parenting role, leading to conflict. In these cases, the time-honoured granny flat may be a godsend.

You may not be quite as desirable as a live-in grandparent as you were as a live-out one. You might snore, leave the bathroom in a mess, drop things, put things away in the wrong place and pass wind at inappropriate moments.

Sometimes there is no choice. One grandparent dies and the other just isn't coping living alone and has nowhere else to go. Or, if you're in that situation, you may decide to take a new partner, something which might cause your children anxiety as they may start to wonder what will happen to their inheritance.

It's worth thinking through what you would do if you were suddenly left alone and couldn't manage by yourself, even though this is an event that may be in the distant future for you. It's smart to anticipate problems. Think of options in advance and sound out your children about what they would honestly prefer. It's always good to set up the rules of engagement from the outset.

Same-sex parents

Since the 1970s, the gay liberation movement has challenged some of the traditional notions about families. About one in 200 Australian families now comprises a same-sex couple. You'll have personal views about this. If you got used to the idea of your child being gay you may have resolved some of your conflicts and be more accepting than the average person.

Some of these conflicts may reappear when your child and partner decide to have children. Grandparents may worry about social stigma against the grandchild. Our society, especially in the larger cities compared with rural areas, is now much more accepting of same-sex relationships but it can still be tough and there are many prejudices. Whether you approve or not, your job is not to make it more difficult for them. It is to be accepting and supportive of your children and your grandchildren.

There are three concerns that you may have for your grandchildren if they are being brought up in a same-sex relationship:

1. That the development of their own sexual identity will be compromised and that they may grow up to be lesbian or gay.
2. That they may have personal development problems, have more behavioural difficulties and be less psychologically healthy than other children.
3. That they will be stigmatised and teased because of their family structure and will have difficulty in their social relationships.

Not surprisingly, a great deal of research has been done in this area. The results may not be in line with some preconceived views, but they strongly suggest that children of same-sex families grow up as well adjusted and with similar sexual orientation as children brought up in traditional families.

Sexual identity

A range of good-quality studies has shown that children of lesbian mothers have been found to be quite happy with the gender they were born with, enjoyed conventional sex roles as they grew up and as adults were no more likely than any other adult to want to be a member of the opposite sex. They enjoyed the same toys and games as children from heterosexual families and were no different in their occupational choices. A range of other studies has failed to show higher rates of homosexuality amongst children of lesbian or gay parents.

Personality and behaviour

As is the case for sexual identity, over 30 studies performed during the last 20 years have shown no major differences in personality development between children of lesbian mothers and children of heterosexual mothers. It's true that there have been fewer studies looking at the children of gay fathers, but in those which had been carried out, there seems to be no evidence for the belief that children of lesbian or gay parents have deficits in their personality development.

Social relationships

Surveys of young adults who grew up with divorced lesbian mothers show that they did not recall any more teasing or stigmatisation than children of divorced heterosexual mothers and their adult romantic relationships were not related to their mothers' sexual orientation.

When relationships with grandparents have been studied, most children of lesbian mothers had regular contact and good relationships with their grandparents.

Whatever we may personally believe about these issues, it's helpful to be aware of the facts; facts which sometimes differ from popular opinion. This is reassuring for grandparents. You may still have to cope with your own feelings, perhaps disappointment, perhaps a little embarrassment and possibly a little guilt, but just treat your grandchildren normally because that's what they are, normal children.

A gay grandchild

Wait a minute, your grandchild has grown up in a heterosexual family. Everything seems to have gone along normally and you've had a great time as a grandparent with your young grandchild. Now it's about 15 years later and you find that your grandchild is gay. What do you do? How do you react? This hasn't happened in your family before.

Hang on a moment, there was Aunt Florence who never married and lived in the Blue Mountains with her female companion Elinor. But surely Elinor was just there to help do some of the secretarial tasks while Aunt Florence was writing her history of the Crimean War. Or was there more to it than that? They were there together for 35 years. It can't take that long to write a history of the Crimean War.

Well, perhaps there has been a hint of it in the family, and if there has been, so what? But what do we do about our grandson? Anyhow, is there any need to do anything? Probably not. A 'good talking to' won't help. He's still our grandson, the one we cuddled and played with and took on outings. He hasn't changed and we mustn't change either. Remember unconditional love? We might have our own views and might feel a little confused. We may or may not approve of the lifestyle, but we can still love the person. He'll need our love and acceptance.

GRANDCHILDREN AND DISABILITY

Your eagerly awaited grandchild has just been born. But there's a problem. The child has a significant disability. It may be obvious at birth if it's a physical disability or if it's a recognised syndrome such as Down syndrome. Or it may take a year or so to become apparent in the case of developmental disability. How do you react? What can you do?

Your own feelings

Grandparents report similar reactions to the birth of a disabled child as parents report. There is shock, sadness about the child's disability, anxiety about her future and sometimes anger. They have been waiting for the 'perfect' grandchild and, instead, a 'less than perfect' one has arrived.

There won't be much professional support available to help you. Many grandparents report that while there is lots of excellent professional support for the parents, and rightly so, professionals often forget to consider the feelings of the grandparents. The good news is that research has shown that the vast majority of grandparents adapt very well to grandchildren with disabilities, love them dearly and value the relationship which develops.

Your child as the parent

You might be surprised, and rather proud, at discovering how well your child and partner cope with a disabled child. Even if they do seem to be doing a good job of managing their emotions and their new, more difficult role, there will still be the need for practical support from you.

I've always been impressed with the parents of my young patients with severe disabilities. In fact, I have been in awe of some of them and often wondered if I would cope nearly as well if I were in their situation.

One patient, Ahmed, was born to an Australian-born mother of Egyptian heritage and a recently immigrated Lebanese father. It wasn't long before it became apparent that little Ahmed was extremely disabled. There were no physical deformities, but his brain just wasn't working properly. He didn't smile, didn't reach his early developmental milestones and had very few reactions or emotions at all. He just remained a very young baby.

On my initial meeting with his mother, I thought that she was unlikely to cope. How wrong I was. She was very strong. She and her husband cared for him and with total devotion even though Ahmed gave little in return, not even smiling. He died when he was just three years old. His parents, who keep in touch with me occasionally, remain a reminder to me that first appearances, and probably my own preconceived ideas, can be deceptive and that parents, as I've seen many times over, often have an inner strength which may only become obvious in tough times.

What can you do?

Parents of disabled children often go through the stages of grief that people go through when a loved one dies. They will need lots of support as well as time. Grandparents can provide practical support, perhaps helping with the other children when hospital visits and doctor's appointments are needed, providing emotional support and acceptance. In many families, grandparents are the main source of support available to parents.

What to avoid

Your job is to be supportive, to give practical help and to love your grandchild, not to interfere, not to become involved in disagreements about how best to care for the child and not to tell the parents how worried you are about the child's future.

If grandparents are still in denial about the disability or the extent of it, if they trawl the internet for simple 'wonder cures' (ones which actually work don't exist) and if they don't really understand the disability and the difficulties faced by the parents and siblings, they are no help at all.

Children with disabilities have personalities and gifts of their own, no matter how severe the disability. It just takes a while to get to know them. They may need more of your time and more patience but, in return, they will give you their love as you give them yours and your life, as well as theirs, will be enriched.

7

Long-distance Grandparenting

You've just become a grandparent. The problem is that your son and daughter-in-law are part way through their five-year contract managing a sheep station in Paraguay. Life wasn't meant to be easy. You are delighted, but you feel a bit let down. You want to visit, give cuddles, be supportive and watch your grandchild grow up.

It's hard being a grandparent when there is a significant geographic distance separating you. It needn't be Paraguay; it might just be that you are separated by a state or live in another part of the state. Wherever the distance may be, you can't just nip over to do a little babysitting or to read the bedtime story.

Why do we move around so much? People move for employment and career opportunities, for financial reasons, sometimes for lifestyle changes and sometimes for health reasons. They may even move to get away from their parents. It's not just the children who move away from their parents. Some grandparents move to warmer climates or join the 'grey nomads' brigade and wander around the country, perhaps deciding to settle at one of the places they see. Others fulfil their dream of retiring, selling up and moving to a new city or a country retreat.

Some families actually get on better with other family members when they are separated by long distances and only see each other occasionally. Whatever the reasons or motivations for moving, distance tends to have an adverse effect on family closeness, particularly the grandparent–grandchild relationship.

For the grandparent–grandchild relationship, distance causes two main problems: not many opportunities for one-on-one time with a grandchild; and an inability to be part of a grandchild's daily life. These aren't insurmountable if some work is put in. Most parents want and encourage a relationship between their children and their own parents and advances in technology make it much easier to stay in touch regularly through a variety of ways.

KEEPING IN TOUCH

It's worth discussing with the parents how best to maintain communication and continuity in a way that suits them, their children and you. Try a few different methods and agree on what works best.

Try to get together at least once a year (a considerable effort if your grandchildren are living in Fairbanks, Alaska, but not quite as hard if they are actually on the same continent as you and more accessible). Agree that when you can get together there will be some one-on-one time with each grandchild. You might have so much to catch up with on your own children that the grandchildren don't really get a chance to know you. Perhaps one of you, grandmother or grandfather, can do some of the catching up with the adults while the other grandparent spends time with the grandchildren, going for a walk, playing make-believe games and reading stories. Then have a turnabout.

You might have to commit some financial resources to this. If your daughter married a merchant banker or a movie star, they may be the ones who pay your airfares and expenses to visit. If she married an out-of-work actor or a street juggler, you may have to pay the expenses not only to visit them, but maybe also for them to make visits to you. If you're having trouble making ends meet as well as your own children not being particularly flush, you might have to start a modest, regular saving plan to ensure that you and your grandchildren can see each other.

It can help if a family photo board is set up at your grandchildren's home. Remember that there will usually be another set of grandparents who are also likely to be long-distance ones, so that they also need to find ways of staying in touch. Some parents put photos of the grandparents, cousins, aunts and uncles on a pin board in a prominent place and regularly point out and name each one to the children, talking with them about them and their families. This gives you an opportunity to regularly send updated photos.

Although the two principles of developing a relationship with grandchildren are one-on-one contact and being part of their daily life, you don't have to have daily contact to be involved in their daily lives and you don't have to have one-on-one contact only at visits. These can both be achieved by regular personal communication using telephone, fax, email, web cameras and even Australia Post.

Phone calls

Have you noticed how the phone tends to ring at the most inconvenient time? Your wife has just slipped out. You've taken the opportunity to settle down on the toilet to read a few more pages of Tolstoy's *War and Peace*. The phone rings. You struggle to answer it, one hand clutching your trousers. It's Mike, whom you've never heard of. He asks, 'How are you today?' You're too polite to tell him how you're actually feeling right at this moment. He then tells you that the Mongolian gerbil is almost extinct but you can make a difference by purchasing a $20 raffle ticket and winning a Mercedes at the same time. You make an appropriate, or perhaps inappropriate, remark and the conversation ends. You return to find that you've lost your place in *War and Peace*.

This might go some way to explain why not every call to your grandchildren is greeted with enthusiastic joy. Telephones are intrusive. It's good to call the grandchildren regularly, but talk with their parents and with them as they become older, about the best times to call. For families who live a long way off, especially if they are on a tight budget, regular calls can be expensive. Your children may be more likely to call you often if you have an 'I'll call you straight back' agreement with them. That way, you'll end up paying for the call, but you may also have much more regular communication.

It's good to call our grandchildren personally, rather than call our children and then at the end of the conversation ask them to say to their child, 'Do you want to speak to Grandma?' Children appreciate their own, personal calls. They may not answer the phone when you call, but you can get straight down to business and just say to your son-in-law, 'Hello Bruno, it's Elva here, can I speak to Michael?' If Michael is expecting a regular call from you, that adds to the enjoyment.

What do you talk about to grandchildren when you are on the telephone? It's not that easy to talk to young children and the call is likely to be quite brief, especially when they decide they have something more interesting to do. Young children will often nod 'yes' to questions on the phone, thinking that you know what they've just done and sometimes they'll show you things. This may make it quite difficult at your end. Don't ask vague questions such as 'How are you today?' Be focused and try, 'Have you had your bath yet?', 'What toys did you play with today?', 'What are you wearing on your feet?' They may try to show you. 'What did you eat for dinner?' They may try to offer you some. Two year olds are smart in many ways, but they don't yet know that telephones have their limits. You can also tell them about anything interesting you did or saw, interesting to them, that is.

You might want to buy older grandchildren a phone card so that they can call you. Conversations with older children can be more interesting, such as talk about school, friends, sports and family. They work better if you stay up to date with what is going on in their lives and follow up on things mentioned in the last phone chat. As mentioned in Chapter 4, keep a notepad by the phone to jot down a few things from a phone conversation so that you can mention them in the next call.

The fax

Do you remember when a fax always had a sense of urgency? In fact most fax cover sheets used to proclaim, in large letters, 'URGENT FAX'. One organisation I know of kept its newly acquired fax machine next to the chief executive's office and a fax could only be sent if the CEO signed an authority for it. How strange. It was only a form of phone call.

Now stand-alone fax machines are almost obsolete. They are just built into computers and printers and no signature is needed to authorise them.

The advantage of a fax for communicating with grandchildren is that it can allow them to fax you drawings they have done at home and at school as well as other messages, cartoons and jokes. You can fax notes, jokes, and cartoons to them, too. 'Okay,' you are saying, 'I have a scanner built into my printer so I can do all of this using my computer.' Do it that way if you like. The point is that a variety of different methods and types of communication keep up interest, for grandparents as well as grandchildren.

Email

Are you computer literate? Your grandchildren will be, so if we grandparents want to use all the available methods of communication, we need to learn to get online. Your grandchildren will enjoy teaching you and helping you to learn new skills and they'll think you're really cool once you've mastered a few.

If you are new to computers and email it may seem daunting at first, but it's easy and the more you do it, the easier it becomes. A word of warning: the computer can be addictive, particularly looking at the vast amount of information on the internet. You don't want your partner to say, 'Are you married to me or to the computer?'

If you live in different time zones, email is a great way to communicate. You can send a brief message, a photo or a cartoon before you go to bed. They are likely to read it while you are asleep and with luck, you'll wake up to find a reply.

Short messages are best and easiest to reply to. Keep them short and send them often. It's a bit of a mindset change. We were brought up thinking that letters usually had to be several pages as we had to buy a stamp for each one. Email is basically free, so there is no need to 'get your money's worth' each time. Just send a one-word sentence, ask a question or send a joke, or a photograph. As some digital cameras are now fairly inexpensive, you may decide to give your grandchild one as a present. Then they can send you photos, too. Or, if your technical skills and manual dexterity are up to it, you may be able to send photos and text messages from your mobile telephone.

If you become really good, or get good advice, you may be able to set up computer games, such as chess, with your grandchildren and play with them online. Distance is no barrier here. Or you may just want to set up a regular time with them when you can chat back and forth for a while on email.

Web cameras

When many grandparents were born the transistor radio had not even been invented. Some of our parents had radios with valves which were housed in polished wooden cabinets with cloth-covered speakers. Television didn't appear in Australia until 1956.

Now you can attach an inexpensive web camera to your computer or your computer may even have one built in. Using a web camera you and your grandchildren can see each other as you talk, even though you may be 15,000 kilometres apart. It's a good way to watch your grandchildren grow (and for them to watch you age), if you don't see each other very often. One colleague of mine described the experience as being too painful. He said his family seemed so close but they couldn't be touched.

Other ideas

You may prefer some of the old technologies and exchange messages and stories on audio tape or perhaps videotape. Remember that chap who calls by each weekday and puts bills and other things into your letterbox? The mail still works and is a great way of communicating. It may also help your grandchildren develop the art of using the brief, handwritten letter, something which may be old-fashioned, but which people still appreciate.

Children like to receive their very own, personal letters, not ones addressed to 'Mr and Mrs Bloggs and family' or even ones addressed to 'Mr and Mrs Bloggs, Matilda and Ebony Bloggs'. Matilda will want one addressed simply to 'Matilda Bloggs'. Ebony will want her own too. Personal letters make children feel special. Send them when they are *not* having a birthday. Spontaneous letters and occasional spontaneous gifts in the mail are often more valued than cards and gifts sent on birthdays, when they are expected.

Spontaneous, random acts of kindness are good as long as they aren't so random that they reach some of your grandchildren but not the others. Letters are best kept short, especially for young children. Send postcards or pictures with a note written on them. There is no rule that postcards only have to be sent by people having fun on holidays to people who are stuck at home, perhaps not having as much fun. A quick note on a postcard can be sent off at any time.

And don't be surprised if your grandchildren don't write back. They may write to you at times and you can make it easier for them by sending them notepaper and stamped envelopes, but the last thing you want is for them to feel a reply is a chore. Letter-writing needs to be spontaneous and fun.

Of course, in all of these forms of communication with distant grandchildren, we need to keep up with their interests so that we can have useful, interesting communication with them. This means we may have to take on new interests ourselves. If your nine-year-old

...don't be surprised if your grandchildren don't write back

grand-daughter plays netball and also follows the fortunes of the Australian netball team, her grandparents, who may previously have known nothing about netball, will have to bone up on the game and also follow the fortunes of the Australian team. You may want to follow your grandson's favourite football team, or, if you want animated discussions, learn about his team but follow an opposing team. In the process, grandparents learn new things as well.

If you send a postcard every Tuesday, it tends to become a bit of a bore for everyone. So vary the forms of communication. Use the phone, the computer, the fax, letters and all the other methods at different times to keep up the interest. Depending on how you wish to communicate with each other, you'll find some more useful than others, but use a variation from time to time.

Here are some fun activities to do with your grandchildren.

The add-on story
You can start off a story by email, perhaps the first one or two sentences and ask your talented grandchild to add the next couple of sentences. You then do the following sentence or two and so on until a short (perhaps very short) story is complete.

The add-on picture
Perhaps a little harder to do by email, unless your computer skills are well above average, but easy to do by mail. Just draw a couple of lines, mail them to your grandchild to add a few more and send the drawing back and forth until you end up with some sort of a picture. It may end up as a picture of a Bunyip, which could be very valuable, as no-one has ever seen one.

The alphabet story
This is sometimes used in theatre workshops to encourage quick, creative thinking but it can work via email too. You think of a scenario—for example, you've just come back to your car to find a police officer issuing a parking ticket. The exchange between you and the police officer has to have the first letter of the first word in each exchange start with the next letter of the alphabet. Confusing isn't it? Here's an example:

YOU: 'Are you booking me?'

POLICE OFFICER: 'Bet your life I am.'

YOU: 'Can't you give me a break? I just stopped outside the hospital to rush in my wife who's about to have a baby.'

POLICE OFFICER: 'Doesn't matter to me sir, you're illegally parked.'

YOU: 'Ever heard of compassion, officer? I'll do anything to have you overlook this.'

POLICE OFFICER: 'Forget it, mate. I'm incorruptible.'

And so on…

Hide and seek from a distance

You can do this after a visit or with the cooperation of the parents by phone or email. Hide (or organise to have hidden) some small treats or gifts in a few places around the house and then send your grandchildren clues over the phone or by email to help them find them.

For grandchildren who are stars

You can have a star named after each of them. Sydney Observatory has a 'name a star' program where you can purchase the naming rights for a real star. And you don't have to live in Sydney to do it. That name is then placed in the official star catalogue and carries the name you chose forever. You might choose Tim the Terrific, Priscilla the Peacemaker, Gloria the Grumpy, Bumptious Bertie or any other name which you think will describe and delight your grandchildren for the rest of their lives.

VISITS

If you and your grandchildren live a long way from each other, visits are much anticipated and potentially very exciting. We all want them to go well. The problem is that when expectations are high, things occasionally don't go as well as we had, perhaps somewhat unrealistically, hoped. But with realistic expectations, flexibility and good humour, things usually work out pretty well and you'll spend the next few weeks after they leave reminiscing about the cute things they did or said.

There are three types of visits: where the family visits you, where just the grandchildren visit you, and where you visit your grandchildren and their parents.

Mum, dad and the kids come to your place

As mentioned in Chapter 4, it's a good idea to plan ahead for the visit. You'll have to decide on a number of things before they arrive.

Where will they stay?

The first thing to decide is where they will stay. This may pose a problem if you downsized when your children moved out, as there may not be room. Options are: for them to stay with you in rooms of their own complete with en-suite, if you have that sort of place; squeeze into every available space including mattresses on the floor and the garage; let them move into a nearby friend's place which you're minding while they are on holiday, having first checked with your friends that it's okay if you wish the friendship to continue; let them stay at your place and you move into your friend's house; put them all up at a nearby bed-and-breakfast or motel; you move into the bed-and-breakfast or motel while they occupy your place; just have the grandchildren at your place and have their parents stay at the motel. You may be able to think of other options.

Childproof your home

If your grandchildren are toddlers, this is an important safety measure (see Chapter 10) and if you have small treasures you don't want smashed, chewed or inhaled, it's wise to have them out of the way, too.

So here's a challenge: get those grandparent knees bending, pull in the stomach, put on your glasses to make sure you don't miss anything and get down on your hands and knees on the floor. This gives you a child's eye view of the world. Now crawl around the house looking for potential hazards. You might find this posture undignified, but being a good grandparent involves being undignified for a lot of the time. Chances are that, as a result of this exercise, you'll find a few potentially dangerous things like paper clips, cockroaches (dead cockroaches aren't really dangerous, but definitely unaesthetic) and a few things under the lounge or bed that you thought you'd lost.

Rules and discipline

It's your house, so your rules should apply. If you don't think jumping on the lounge in muddy shoes is a good idea, don't allow it. It's the parents' job to ensure that their children stick to your rules, providing, of course, that your rules are reasonable. But as for methods of discipline, that's up to the parents. Grandparents just have to be supportive and take care not to do anything that undermines the parents' authority.

How long will the visit last?

Let's be honest. Having grandchildren and the family stay can be great fun. For weeks after they leave you'll be recalling some of the cute things they did and said. But it can also be a strain, and not just for you. They'll feel it too.

You've got used to being a couple who are home alone and who can use their time pretty much as they like. You've also probably got into a routine, perhaps even a rut. As we become older we tend to become a little less tolerant and a little less flexible, not just in our joints. Part of the job of visits with grandchildren is to get grandparents out of the rut, and increase our tolerance and flexibility. It's good for us, but it can be stressful at times and rather tiring, particularly if it's a fairly lengthy visit of several weeks.

Remember that on these visits you don't have to be with them *all* the time. Take some time out for yourself. Go for a walk, do some shopping, have coffee with a friend. That way you will feel refreshed and your children will probably appreciate the break, too.

Looking after mum and dad

When the family visits it's a good opportunity for grandparents to look after the parents as well as the grandchildren. They'll appreciate having their meals cooked (well, that depends on what the cooking is like) and being 'mothered and fathered' a little themselves. After all, they're still our children. At home they may not have the chance to get out alone very often. Grandparents can mind the grandchildren while the parents go out for a meal, a movie, a live show or just have time to do some shopping in freedom.

When they've all gone home, you may be able to sleep in again, read the paper in peace and clean away the grubby finger marks. It will be quieter and far less exciting, but it will give you time to start planning their next visit.

The grandchildren come to stay

Your grandchildren are likely to be excited when they arrive. They'll have lots of energy and expect you to have lots of energy, too. You'll need to plan ahead and get things ready before they arrive.

When the grandchildren visit without their parents, finding space is less of a problem. The options of putting them up at the motel, a bed-and-breakfast or an absent friend's home aren't really on. You'll need to childproof the house if they are toddlers (see Chapter 10), get in a stock of their favourite breakfast cereals and other foods and give some thought to what you can do together. It's wise to discuss some of these plans with their parents just to make sure they approve, particularly if bungee jumping or hang-gliding are on your proposed list of activities.

Younger children like security and rituals so it's worth checking with their parents about bedtime routines, food likes and dislikes as well as what rules the parents think are important. They may miss their parents, particularly at bedtime or when things aren't going well, so find opportunities to stay in touch with their parents by phone and perhaps email as well.

You'll need to plan some outings that don't have to be elaborate and where you build in enough flexibility to alter them if there are problems with the weather for outdoor activities.

Make sure you take plenty of photos so you can let their parents have some (you can send them by email now that you've mastered this skill) to reassure them that things are going well. The grandchildren can also take some photos home to remind them of the good times and make them keen to visit you again.

Where will they sleep?

Choose somewhere safe without access to staircases and balconies (see Chapter 10 on childproofing the house).

A portable cot is a good investment. It can either stay at your place for visits from various grandchildren or, if you are lucky to have your children living nearby, they can bring it over when they visit and need to put the baby down for a sleep. Just make sure it conforms to Australian standards, is secure and won't collapse. You might have an old cot in the garage or attic you decide to use. Perhaps the one your children used. You need to make sure that it complies with current standards so that there is no gap between the mattress and the cot sides and that the distance between the cot bars is between 5 and 8.5 centimetres.

A night-light may help your grandchildren feel more secure. Make sure they bring their favourite soft toy with them. If it's something they need to help them get off to sleep at home, they will certainly need it when sleeping at their grandparents' place. It's often helpful to have an intercom set up in their bedroom so that you can hear any cries of distress from whatever part of the house you may be relaxing (or recovering) in once they've gone to bed. Then when you go to bed, set it up in your bedroom. Make sure that you set it up correctly so you can hear sounds coming from their room but they can't hear sounds coming from yours, just in case you have enough energy left to get up to any tricks of your own.

What will they eat?

A visit to the grandparents isn't the opportunity to correct all of their eating habits that you secretly disapprove of. Do some shopping in advance, buy their favourite foods and let them enjoy their meals. Just remember that with many young children, mealtimes are interruptions to their play so don't be surprised if the meals aren't the highlight of their stay.

Many grandchildren like to have their own special mug, plate or cutlery and grandparents often find it helpful to keep a set for each child for when they visit. This also helps give the child a sense of security and stability. Whether it helps them eat better, I have no idea. Other grandchildren might like to choose the plate they will use and the cup they will drink from if you have a range of coloured plastic ones.

You know all this already, but just as a reminder, it's better to give young children plastic drinking cups rather than glasses. They bounce when they are dropped on the floor, rather than shattering into tiny, dangerous pieces. You'll also remember from past experience that it's best not to fill the drink to the top. Half a cup of chocolate milk spilt on the floor isn't as messy as a full cup, so fill it up halfway. If they drink it all you can give them the other half.

Young children regard nearly all food as finger food, so it's okay to let them eat with their fingers. They will probably eat more that way, and instead of washing up their cutlery you'll only have to wipe their fingers, and perhaps yours too.

You probably know whether or not the children eat with their parents at home. This depends on the age of the children and parent schedules. If you can, encourage them to sit at the table and eat with you, without the television on, even if you have to have your meal a little earlier. There is some recent research about the value of family meals. You might want to pass it on to your children if you can do it without harassing them about it. You could always highlight the following paragraph and leave this book open in a conspicuous place.

A recent survey found that 50 per cent of Australian families now eat their dinner sitting in front of a television set. There is now hard evidence that this isn't good for their children. A study from Harvard University found that children who eat dinner with their families, in the absence of television, develop better language skills than other children. Another study from Columbia University in New York, found that children who ate meals with their families were less likely to become involved with drugs and alcohol and even scored better marks at school. So here is an opportunity for grandparents to do some role modelling.

Of course, the sit-down family meal with the grandchildren has to be fun for them. Talk to them about themselves and their family. Plan the next day's activities. Find out more about school or preschool. Just resist the temptation to nag them about eating all of their vegetables. They won't die of scurvy or beriberi if they don't have top-class nutrition for a few days, but they will benefit from the ritual of the family having a meal together.

How will you fill in the day?

Children enjoy outings but the visit needn't be one continuous round of organised activities. Children just like time when they can be unorganised and play by themselves. Just as well, too. This is your chance to recover, perhaps do a little cleaning up and to prepare for whatever the next activity might be. Be flexible. Plans may have to change because of the weather, the child not being interested, or even because what you've planned just doesn't seem to be working. Remember that young children have short attention spans so that complex or long activities may lose their appeal quite quickly. It's good to check your plans with the parents to make sure they approve of them and to see if they have any advice to offer.

Remember, children like rituals. You may find that when they come to visit you they like to do the same things as on the last visit: to go to the same place; play the same games; watch the same DVD and involve you in the same imaginative game they roped you into the last time.

Depending on their age, simple activities are often the most enjoyable: going to the park; going on a nature walk and looking for flowers or beetles or for the tallest tree or having a picnic lunch in the backyard. Here are some suggestions:

- Get them to do some jobs. Young children like to help. Of course the job may take longer with them helping and they may tire of helping long before the job is finished, but it can be fun for you and them. It also helps them to burn up energy, which has two good results—it makes them hungry so mealtime is more likely to be a success, and it makes them tired so that they will be more likely to sleep well (as will you).

  They can help with cleaning, washing the car and if you're game, gardening. Many horticulturally challenged adults can't tell the difference between a garden plant and a weed, so it's unrealistic to expect a grandchild to be able to do this.

This can be solved by giving them an area of the garden
to work in where not much damage can be done and
where you can give specific tasks, such as digging a hole,
searching for worms, collecting different-coloured leaves or
pulling up weeds.

- Play games. You don't have to think up all the games
  yourself and they do need time just to play alone, but
  they also appreciate imaginative grandparents who can
  suggest ideas for games. Some of your ideas may go down
  like the proverbial lead balloon, but occasionally one may
  strike a chord and you're off and away. A dress-up box
  full of old clothes is often a great success. You may want
  to suggest blowing bubbles, painting on butcher's paper
  with watercolours, drawing on a blackboard, playing
  shops, playing astronauts or playing hide and seek.
  Board games are good for older children (yes, they still
  exist despite the computer age) who often love them
  because they are different.

  You can even plan a backwards afternoon where you all
  say 'goodbye' instead of 'hello', 'yes' instead of 'no', walk
  backwards and put on clothes back-to-front. Just let your
  partner know what you plan to do, otherwise you might find
  that the guys in white coats have been called.

- Play in the kitchen. Little children love to play in the
  kitchen if that's where the grandparents are for some of the
  time. The kitchen is a potentially hazardous place, so make
  sure that the cupboard under the sink has nothing
  dangerous in it, such as drain cleaner and that sharp objects
  and electrical cords are out of reach. Be very careful with
  boiling water to avoid accidental scalds. You might want to
  fill a low kitchen drawer or a cupboard with things that are
  safe, not precious and which the child can pull out and play
  with; such as wooden spoons, measuring cups and plastic
  food containers.

- Cooking together. Young children love to cook. It doesn't
  have to be cordon bleu; it just has to be something where
  you and your grandchild can be involved and where they can

feel that they have made something wonderful. If you decide to make a cake or some biscuits:

— Use a recipe which is simple and which you know will work.
— Get the ingredients and utensils out in advance.
— Let the child put the ingredients in the mixing bowl and mix them together; this will depend on the child's age and skills and you may need to help them.
— Let your grandchild lick the bowl and utensils. Some may want to do this even before they finish mixing.
— If making biscuits, they can cut out shapes with a cookie cutter and put a Smartie or M&M on the top. They'll certainly want to sample the sweet first to make sure it's okay to apply to the biscuit. Let them do it. It's all part of the fun.
— Do all this at child height on a low table or even on the floor.
— Use the opportunity to teach them to be aware of a hot oven.
— Freshly baked food tastes best. They'll want to try some as soon as it's out of the oven and cooled. They'll love taking a small container of their biscuits or a slab of their cake home as a gift for their parents.

Visiting your children and grandchildren

If it's a long journey, perhaps to the opposite side of Australia, or to another country, you'll arrive tired as well as emotional. But remember that it is likely to be full-on from the moment you arrive. After all, the grandchildren haven't seen you in a while. There may be a little initial caution and hesitancy on the part of the younger ones until they feel comfortable with you, but after that you'll be a pushover and you'll love it.

Where will you stay?

It's not much fun living out of a suitcase in the living room for a week or more. Unless there is plenty of space, it may be better to stay at a nearby hotel, motel or bed-and-breakfast. This gives you extra privacy, some wind-down time and saves you from being underfoot all the time. The parents might appreciate this, too.

Bringing gifts

You'll probably want to bring some presents for the grandchildren. They are always appreciated so long as they are similar in interest and value. You don't want to have one grandchild immediately won over and the others alienated. Remember that one of the parents is your child too and that all children appreciate presents!

It's not your place

Grandparents who stay with their children for a visit are their guests. This means we don't act like parents and takeover: constantly tidying up; wiping away finger marks that might have been there for weeks and fixing things which don't need fixing. It is fine to help and we should, but we haven't come to be critical, to take over and to get up the noses of own child and our daughter-in-law or son-in-law. We've come to catch up with our children, to get to know our grandchildren better, to have some precious one-on-one time with them and to share in their daily lives.

Sharing in their daily lives is good for them as well as for us and will give us lots of good memories. We can get involved in taking them to school, helping with homework if needed, reading bedtime stories, bathing, meeting their friends, hearing about their hobbies, teaching them things and letting them teach us things. After we've gone, our increased knowledge of their daily lives will give our phone calls, emails and letters much more substance.

Look after your children too

If you are a guest, your children will be looking after you. You can also help look after them. Send them out to dinner or a movie one night while you babysit. Mind the children while they go shopping. Buy them a gift that you think they might like, or better still, find out what they would really like and buy them that. Offer to cook a meal, do some jobs that they really want done, or do the shopping, but all in a way that helps, rather than takes over.

Awkward, unexpected situations

We are likely to have high expectations for the visit, but what if we find that we have arrived at a difficult time, or if the situation has changed and we don't know about it?

Father, the main breadwinner, has lost his job the day before you arrived. Your divorced daughter now has a new boyfriend and you find that he's just moved in. You notice that your daughter's upper arms are bruised and you suspect domestic violence. You become concerned when you notice how much and how often one of the parents 'needs a drink'. Is there a serious drinking problem you didn't know about?

You know that the parents have separated but what you find out when you visit is that there is an unpleasant custody battle with accusations and counter-accusations being made by both parents and with your grandchildren suffering as they are caught up in this unpleasantness.

What do you do? Pretend nothing is happening and that it's one big, happy family? Pack your bags and go home in a huff? Immediately take sides and jump to conclusions? Your own emotions will surface. You may be confused, angry, embarrassed and have feelings of guilt and powerlessness. You might be tempted to point out what you've 'always suspected' or what you predicted years ago. You may be tempted, but don't give in. And don't nag.

There are no easy answers. Depending on the problem, professional help may be needed. It helps to take a cold, hard look at the emotions you may be experiencing and work out which ones are going to be counter-productive because they involve 'me' and then think about how you can be helpful, rather than add to the family's problems.

This is where your hopefully well-honed skills of tolerance and understanding, of being a good listener rather than a good talker, and of empathy rather than self-centredness will be needed. Above all, your grandchildren may need your support and, depending on their age, your advice. You'll need to do this mostly in a way which is consistent with the parents' values and doesn't undermine their authority. In a time of family disruption, grandparents, even long-distance ones if they keep in touch regularly, can be an important element of stability for their grandchildren.

You can also give practical support. Financial help if that's what's needed (if you can do it) and also on the visit you can offer to take the grandchildren out more or find other ways of spending extra time with them so as to give their parents a little more space to work through their issues.

How long should you stay?

The best type of meal is one where we savoured every delicious mouthful, have just finished and feel we would like just a little more. The worst sort of meal is where we enjoy it, then stuff ourselves with more than we need and feel uncomfortable afterwards. Visits are the same. Don't overdo them. Plan to stay not too long so that you'll be missed when you leave and your return visit will be eagerly anticipated. That's far better than having your children dropping hints, offering to help pack your bags and checking to see if an earlier flight is available.

8

When Grandparents Do the Parenting

You've worked hard, raised your children and have become a grandparent. All of a sudden, you find that you have been asked to take responsibility for the full-time, long-term care of your grandchildren. Perhaps just the one, or possibly three or four, or even more. You have to start all over again.

All of those clichés about 'being able to give them back' are no longer true. You're still a grandparent and you'll try to do a good job as a full-time carer for your grandchildren, but the special joys and relationship of being a grandparent aren't quite the same. Your dreams of more freedom, opportunities to travel and more time with friends suddenly all evaporate. The plans to do things together as a couple won't work now. You have a full-time, unpaid job and you have less energy than 25 or 30 years ago.

The grandchildren who move in with you may have behavioural problems if they have had a rough time and will need more attention than usual. They may be rebellious or resentful as a result of the events which led to their being put into your care. They may feel fragile and rejected and, if so, will need a lot of time, care and perhaps some additional professional support. You will have to exert discipline and at the same time cope with changed societal expectations about child-rearing.

Wow! What a change of lifestyle. You'll still love them and care for them and they will give you a lot of pleasure, but life has suddenly become very different for all of you.

WHY DOES THIS HAPPEN?

Paula and Michael had left their 18-month-old daughter with Paula's parents while they went back to Canberra, where they first met, to celebrate their fourth wedding anniversary over the weekend. Young Tanya was indulged by her grandparents Dimitra and Con, as only grandparents can, and the three of them had a wonderful weekend.

Paula and Michael lashed out on an expensive hotel, had a romantic dinner and savoured the rare pleasure of just being alone together.

Then, driving home the next day, at a set of traffic lights only 5 kilometres from home, a truck came through a red light at high speed and slammed into their car. Michael was killed instantly. Paula survived the crash but died in hospital. Michael's parents weren't in a situation where they could provide full-time care for orphaned Tanya and there were no other relatives willing to take on this role, so the bulk of the responsibility for raising Tanya throughout her childhood fell on Paula's parents. They did a good job, but it was certainly different from their idea of what life would be like for them as grandparents.

Tragic situations such as this are not very common. Grandparents usually assume full-time care of their grandchildren for quite different reasons.

The transition from a regular grandparent to a grandparent who does the parenting sometimes does not come as a surprise. Quite often grandparents are usually aware of problems such as alcohol abuse, drug abuse, mental illness or intellectual disability which may lead to the point where the parents can no longer provide adequate care.

A patient of mine, Liam, had just turned two and was the youngest of three boys. He had been born prematurely with a heart problem requiring complex surgery and so had spent his early weeks in the Children's Hospital. After that he continued to come back regularly for further assessment and treatment.

Greg and Kelly, his parents, were heroin addicts. The three boys had been cared for by various relatives at different times of crisis or when their parents were unable to provide adequate care, including a period when Greg had been briefly in prison. Most of this care had been provided by Kelly's parents.

When Kelly called the Children's Hospital one day to say that Liam was vomiting profusely, we were concerned that there may have been a serious problem and asked them to bring Liam straight to the hospital. When an hour had passed and Liam's parents still hadn't arrived, one of our nurses went outside to look around. There in a car parked outside the emergency department were Greg and Kelly, seemingly unconscious in the car, with Liam, covered in vomit and whimpering in the rear car seat. Apparently Greg and Kelly had decided to 'shoot up' before bringing Liam into the emergency department. As a result of this episode, which was the culmination of several other concerning events, the appropriate authorities were notified and the Children's Court removed Liam from his parents' care, giving custody of all three children to Greg's parents.

Situations like that of Greg and Kelly are more common as causes of grandparents taking on a parenting role than are out-of-the-blue accidents as in Paula and Michael's case.

It is becoming more common

Although grandparents have always had a role in raising grandchildren throughout the ages, in Australia and other developed countries there is a rapid rise in the number of grandparents raising their grandchildren. This increase is largely due to illicit drug use by the parents of the grandchildren. Children of parents with substance abuse problems make up the largest group of children entering the child welfare system. In the United States, the number of children being raised by grandparents has increased by 78 per cent in the last 10 years, with 72 per cent of grandparents raising their grandchildren because of maternal drug abuse. An Australian audit of children in formal kinship care found that 52 per cent of their parents were substance abusers.

The situation is much more common than most people think. There are over 22,000 families in Australia comprising grandparents raising grandchildren. This represents 1 per cent of Australian families. And, of course, grandparents aren't young. In 60 per cent of these families, the grandparents are aged over 55. Almost two-thirds of these grandparent families rely on some sort of government benefit or pension for their income. Children who live with their grandparents often still maintain contact with their parents, with about 70 per cent having regular contact.

There are potential financial difficulties. Grandparent families are poorer on average than most other families. In addition to those trying to manage on government benefits, 47 per cent of grandparent families comprise single grandparents without a partner. As a result, many children living with grandparents are also financially disadvantaged. In fact, this large group of grandparents raising grandchildren has become a new group of disadvantaged Australians.

There are three different ways for grandparents to be given responsibility for their children:

1. A parenting order from the Commonwealth Family Court

It is becoming more common for the Family Court to give custody to grandparents if it decides that this is in the child's best interests. In making such a decision, the Court will consider the nature of the relationship between the child and the grandparents, the capacity of the grandparents to provide for the needs of the child, whether the grandparents already have a significant role caring for the child and the likely effect on the child of being separated from an involved grandparent.

Roxanne was a single mother with a seven-year-old son, Kelvin. There had been no contact with Kelvin's father since the pregnancy and his whereabouts were unknown. When Roxanne was 22, she was diagnosed with schizophrenia. It was a stormy illness and her parents looked after Kelvin whenever Roxanne was not managing or when she found some part-time work. They also often looked after him on weekends.

When Roxanne was taking her medication she managed quite well, but in the last eight months there had been several occasions when she decided she no longer needed her medication, with disastrous results. On the last occasion she disappeared for two days, leaving Kelvin alone in the house. Roxanne's parents decided that Kelvin was just not safe enough and applied to the Family Court for a parenting order. Roxanne did not contest the application and Kelvin was placed in his grandparents' care with the Family Court allowing regular contact with Roxanne, although it was now Roxanne's parents who had the legal responsibility for Kelvin's care, schooling and any medical treatment.

Grandparents who are given custody through a Family Court order become eligible for Family Tax benefits. They may also be eligible for other benefits provided through Centrelink, but these benefits are means tested.

2. A Care and Protection Order through a Children's Court

In the case of Liam and his brothers, the child protection authorities were notified by the Children's Hospital when he was found in his parents' car. This resulted in the Children's Court making a Care and Protection Order, and placing him in the care of Greg's parents. From a financial point of view, this arrangement is less of a burden for the grandparents as they receive non-taxable, non-means tested payments to help with the costs of caring for the children.

3. Informal arrangements

When Paula and Michael died in the car accident, the rest of the family decided, and Paula's parents agreed, that 18-month-old Tanya already had a close relationship with Paula's parents, Dimitra and Con, and so they assumed custody.

Informal arrangements can also be put in to place and agreed to by families in a variety of circumstances, such as a single mother who is too young to manage alone, parents who have intellectual disability, or as a temporary arrangement during a period when parents are not coping.

Families sometimes prefer informal arrangements—for example, if the grandparents are reluctant to seek a formal legal order from the Family Court in case it antagonises or upsets the parents, or because the legal process is too costly for them. Informal arrangements can pose problems when it comes to such things as obtaining a Medicare card, giving consent for medical treatment and in enrolling the child in school, because grandparents in this situation do not have any legal authority to do these things.

BEING A PARENTING GRANDPARENT

If you are a grandparent in this situation you may experience a wide range of feelings as well as some frustrations. These can include:

- feelings of inadequacy that you may not be able to do the job well
- grief about the situation with your own children, which led to your new role
- anger about this change to your planned lifestyle
- uncertainty about appropriate discipline for your grandchildren because of changing views in society
- worry about your capacity to continue in this new role for what may be 10 or 15 years or even longer
- conflict with your children, the natural parents
- difficulties in relationships with your partner brought on or exacerbated by these new stresses
- coping with some of the anger that your other children may feel because you now lack the time to fulfil the traditional grandparenting role for your other grandchildren
- frustration because you may have been given the care of your grandchildren but not the authority to make important decisions
- tension over indulging your grandchildren on the one hand and being responsible for their discipline and a whole range of parenting tasks on the other
- worry about your own health and what may happen to your grandchildren if you become ill, incapacitated or die.

That's quite a list. Of course you may experience only some of these feelings and they may be transient. You will also be likely to have many positive experiences with your grandchildren, which will make your new role very fulfilling. You will also need to be aware of your own health needs, the potential danger of your new role for isolating you from some of your friends (as you now have less time) and the need to seriously look after yourself.

In 2003, the Federal government, with the help of COTA National Seniors (COTA stands for Council of the Ageing), commissioned a survey of grandparents who were raising grandchildren. Four hundred and ninety-nine grandparents (63 per cent were couples), raising a total of 548 grandchildren, participated. Two-thirds of the grandparents were 55 years or older. The oldest was an 82-year-old grandmother who was raising three teenagers on her own. More than half of the grandchildren were less than 10 years old. One grandchild was only three months old. The survey asked about problems the grandparents had encountered in legal and financial matters and in providing parenting for their grandchildren. They were then asked to talk about how they were dealing with these issues and what they needed to help them deal with them more effectively.

Irrespective of where they lived or their socio-economic circumstances, the grandparents told similar stories, and their stories were very similar to what had been found in earlier overseas studies. They recounted their hardships, but they were also quick to say that they loved their grandchildren and would do whatever was required to protect them and nurture them. They also pointed out that their grandchildren brought them great joy and kept them active. Their stories told of endurance, hardship and love.

YOUR HEALTH AND WELLBEING

Some grandparents who take on the care of their grandchildren suffer from depression and anxiety and have more physical health problems than grandparents enjoying the more traditional role. This may be related to increased tiredness, disappointment, anger, frustration and the whole range of feelings outlined above.

Physical health can also suffer if we become tired and overworked and don't have the time to look after our own health, particularly as we are now at the age when health problems become more common. Chapter 9 outlines some ways of making sure you can maintain your health.

Emotional health

There is the risk of becoming isolated from friends and peers if we are no longer free to participate in their interests and enjoy activities with them. Friends and even family may not offer very much help because they may not be sure of what to do, or because they don't understand the implications of our new situation. Or some of us may just be too independent, proud or stubborn to ask for help. The extra duties we've taken on will often mean that there will not be as many opportunities to spend time with our other children and their children. For some, there may even be feelings of shame or embarrassment because of being seen to have a dysfunctional family.

In some cases, even our friends may lose interest in having us over to social functions because we now have children with us and we may not be in a financial position to have a regular, trusted and reliable babysitter.

Here are some comments from the government survey mentioned earlier. One grandparent couple, aged 67 and 61, caring for grandchildren aged five and seven said: 'Socially we have suffered, as we see a lot of younger parents who don't relate to us…also our own age group does not relate to our situation. Our own adult children are disinterested in helping us, and are under enough stress of their own. They are also angry with their sibling who is the mother of the kids and this has created a family rift.'

However, it's not all doom and gloom. One grandmother, aged 60, found great support from a grandparenting group: 'The grandparent group has been a godsend as it has helped me no end'.

One grandparent couple aged 47 and 49, caring for seven- and eight-year-old grandchildren, were unable to find any support, so they took the initiative: 'One day I found another parent like us. We started talking in depth and I found out there was a group in the Southern Highlands called "Off Our Rockers". I got into contact with this group and then decided that a group like this should be started in the Illawarra as there was no support for grandparents with their grandchildren. I approached Jane (Salvation Army officer) and together we started our own group. We had no funding from anybody. I started by advertising in the local papers and sent letters to every school in the Illawarra, also the community centres and preschools, all at my own expense. From there we started getting other people ringing in and coming to our meetings.'

There may also be other family pressures. As well as having less time for your other children and other grandchildren, some grandparents in their forties and fifties still have a child of their own at home.

You may also have an important role in caring for your own elderly parents, so that there are three generations of family which you feel responsible for.

Physical health

Looking after yourself and each other is essential, even though it may seem like a luxury in terms of time and money. If you're in that 63 per cent of grandparents raising children who are a couple, you need to work on supporting each other by:

- sharing the load so that you can each have some personal time out
- making an appointment with your family doctor. Explain the family situation. Have a check-up and follow through on any resources or supports that are recommended
- trying to get some regular exercise by yourself. Walking is simple and particularly helpful
- seeing if you can get a brief quiet time each day which is yours. Have a nap, listen to music or read. You may think it's self-indulgent when there is so much to do. Think of it as an investment for your grandchildren, your family and yourself. You can't keep running on empty.

When Dimitra and Con suddenly found themselves in a full-time parenting position for their 18-month-old grand-daughter Tanya, they experienced a range of emotions. There was intense grieving for the sudden loss of Paula and Michael in a car accident without the opportunity to even say goodbye or to tell them all the things they had meant to tell them one day, but had never got around to doing.

Con had been planning to retire in two years but had to delay these plans because of the extra costs associated with caring for Tanya, particularly as Dimitra had to give up her part-time job. Dimitra found caring for Tanya to be exhausting as well as rewarding and was reluctant to be parted from her at all in the early months of caring for her.

They were also angry about the accident, about the truck driver who had killed their children and, although they didn't admit it openly, they were angry about this change to their lifestyle when they had been looking forward to having more time as a couple, having fewer responsibilities, sleeping in more often and travelling overseas occasionally. They were also worried if they could still do a good job as parents.

They had two other adult children, both of whom had children of their own and they wondered how they could ever find enough time to be good grandparents to these other grandchildren. To top it off, Con's family doctor had recommended he have an annual screening test for bowel cancer and this year the stool sample showed some blood, which meant Con would have to have some investigations and surgery if cancer was found. He knew that screening tests save lives by detecting cancer early but for him, this result had come at a bad time.

The early weeks were a whirlwind of activity accompanied by seesawing emotions, while all the time they did their very best to have a calm, regular routine for Tanya, accompanied by lots of hugs and cuddles. They were fortunate that their family rallied to provide support. Michael's parents offered to have Tanya on alternate weekends, something Tanya enjoyed and which gave Con and Dimitra a chance to recoup, to catch up on other jobs, to go to the movies together at times and to have the occasional luxury of not having to get up too early in the morning. Their other adult children took Tanya during some of the school holidays so that Con and Dimitra did have a few opportunities to travel.

Further investigations showed that Con did have bowel cancer and required prompt surgery. Fortunately, the screening test had detected it at an early stage, the surgeon was able to remove the cancer completely and Con made a total recovery. The operation did occur at a time when the other set of grandparents were away, but one of Dimitra's other children took Tanya for two weeks which also ensured that Tanya was able to visit her grandfather in hospital.

The COTA survey revealed some of the difficulties other grandparents faced. 'It took its toll on my marriage—my husband has left me. It's hard doing it by myself, especially when he's been a very caring and loving husband. It became very stressful on him. He did a lot of overtime. It is also affecting my job as I need to be away from home for two to three nights. They get sick and I take time off work, when we only get three days' parenting leave per year,' said a 49-year-old grandmother caring for her three- and six-year-old grandchildren.

Another grandparent couple, aged 57 and 55, who were given custody of their two grandchildren said: 'The younger boy (now seven) has a low level of ADD, his behaviour is quite good most of the time, however he has had some problems with his progress at school and is repeating...they are both very special to us and we love them dearly and we do our best to help them to develop into good citizens.'

Others were confident that they were doing a good job and that their grandchildren were flourishing. A 72-year-old grandmother caring for grandchildren aged nine and 15 said about one of them: 'Actually the child is much better off with me, top of the class at school, attending the cubs, church and swimming.'

One grandparenting couple interviewed for the COTA survey summed it up when they spoke of the three grandchildren they cared for, aged two, 11 and 14: 'We wouldn't part with these kids. They are our life. They are good kids.'

...may have been exposed to criminal behaviour

YOUR GRANDCHILD'S HEALTH AND WELLBEING

If your grandchild has suddenly lost both parents through a tragic accident, this will need to be worked through. There is some information in Chapter 6 on the stages of grieving which people go through and the support needed.

However, the majority of children who are placed in the care of their grandparents have been exposed to a variety of problems in their own families which may have already compromised their emotional health. Some will have been physically, emotionally or sexually abused or will have been exposed to their parents' drug taking. Others may have experienced a range of family violence. Some may even had to live through the murder of their mother by their father, step-father or their mother's de facto partner. Their parents may have died from a drug overdose. They may have been exposed to criminal behaviour.

Emotional health

Children who grow up amidst disorder, inconsistency, fear and lack of a clear framework for behaviour are likely to have many problems. They are often less advanced in their social development than other children of the same age but may be far more 'streetwise'. They may have difficulty trusting people if their experiences have taught them that the people who they expect to be able to trust often let them down. They may feel bad about themselves, be suspicious of others, difficult to help, be hostile, antisocial or become withdrawn and depressed.

They may have lots of questions. Some may feel responsible for the situation with their parents, feeling that they should have been able to make things better. They may want to talk about their feelings. Let them do it, make it easy for them, but don't push them to talk before they are ready. Answer their questions truthfully, but don't overload them with information. Help them to cope with one thing at a time.

Some are surprisingly resilient. They will all respond to consistency, unconditional love and clear, reasonable boundaries for behaviour. For some, the response may be rapid. For others it may take quite a while and although you'll get there in the end, it's a real challenge for grandparents. You may need some sensible, professional support to guide you through this period.

The following roles are normally those parents would take on, but if the children haven't been helped to develop these skills from their own parents, and as you are now functioning as their parents as well as a grandparent, you may have to start right from the beginning:

- Start simply. Routine household tasks such as tidying the bedroom and putting away the dishes work when they are done in an atmosphere of encouragement and praise. If they don't want to tidy their bedroom, don't make a big issue and waste your emotional energy on it. After all, they are the ones who have to live in it.
- Teach infant school-age children to tell the time. It gives them a sense of achievement and can help them with their routines.
- Be alert to when they are ready to help you in some of your more complex tasks. Give them the opportunity, praise them and thank them.

- You might even be able to teach them how to use the washing machine, dryer or to hang out clothes. This helps foster independence and may be a way of adding a bonus to pocket money.
- Engage them in cooking and enjoy the results with them.
- Teach them about taking responsibility for their actions, not just when things go wrong, but also give them recognition when things go right. Don't make too big a deal about praise, but don't forget it either.
- It generally works out that if you give children responsibility at the level they can manage, they enjoy it and will be keen to take on more responsibility.

When the Children's Court gave custody of Liam and his two brothers to Greg's parents, the children were not at all easy to look after. At times they had been neglected, they had witnessed physical violence between Greg and Kelly and they hadn't been exposed to any consistent, clear rules for behaviour. This made them unruly at times, fearful at other times and often quite unpredictable. Esmay and Daryl had all the mixed emotions which come from suddenly being thrust into a parenting role as well as trying to bring some order and consistency, combined with hefty doses of affection, into the lives of their three grandchildren. They did their best and now, looking back, they can see that they did a reasonably good job, but they needed help. Fortunately, the financial situation was manageable as the government child welfare agency covered medical and other costs for the boys and gave Esmay and Daryl regular payments for the boys' clothing and living expenses. They received excellent support from their local church, had a family doctor who gave them time when they just wanted to talk and referred them to counselling services when they needed further professional help. They received a great deal of help from the charitable organisation Aunties & Uncles, which provided them with family support services. Using a system of volunteers and coordinators, Aunties & Uncles became linked with the family and provided an extended family for the children to trust and rely upon. This included visits and regular weekend outings for the children, which also provided respite for Esmay and Daryl. The coordinators also provided friendship and encouragement for Esmay and Daryl.

The government survey also interviewed grandchildren who were living with their grandparents. These children had been given stability but their lives had changed too.

A 12-year-old boy spoke about missing his friends: 'It's not very cool living with Nan. Nan drives really slowly and she isn't confident driving any more, so we never go very far. My friends don't live close by so I don't get to see them that much...Nan worries about me, she thinks that I will be like my mum and dad, but I won't. I just want to do the stuff other kids do. The good thing is that I get to play footy, so I see my mates then.'

When grandparents take on the parenting role they need to ensure their grandchildren's contact with friends and other relationships are maintained as much as possible.

An 11-year-old girl spoke of what an important figure her grandmother was in providing reliability and stability: 'My Nan and I are working together to build strength in our family. We are there for each other. Sometimes it's hard; sometimes I wish that I lived back with my mum, and that everything was okay, but Nan looks after me. I know that she loves me and I know that Mum cannot look after me. I can rely on Nan.'

Overall, the survey found many problems but also told the remarkable stories of hundreds of grandparents who, while they had little choice, were making their grandchildren's health and happiness their number one priority.

Liam and his brothers responded well to the consistency their new life gave them and after some initial turbulence their behaviour improved. Stephen, the oldest of the three, had been really struggling at school and surprised everyone when his academic skills, as well as his social skills, were seen to improve rapidly over the next 12 months.

Their parents, Greg and Kelly, seemed to have been on a steady downhill progression but the court ordering the removal of their children became a turning point. They entered a rehabilitation program, and despite some initial problems and relapses, they stuck with it and eventually were able to stay clean. After two years they were granted custody of their three boys. Liam continued to be brought back to the Children's Hospital by his parents for regular checks and we were delighted to watch him grow and develop into a healthy, happy, normal boy.

Physical health

As well as general health and nutrition mentioned in Chapter 9, if your grandchild has come from a difficult emotional environment they may have poor physical health as well. They may have had poor nutrition, have been physically injured in the past and may not be up to date with their immunisations. Their teeth may also have been neglected.

It's a good idea to take them to your family doctor for a check-up soon after they come into your care. In addition to a general health review, their immunisation status can be checked and their height and weight measured to see whether they fit within the normal range. If there are concerns about developmental disability, they may need to be referred to a specialist paediatrician. Dental care is expensive, as we all know, but it may be able to be arranged through a dental hospital if finances are tight.

LEGAL CONCERNS

Grandparents and the children they are caring for may become caught up in what to them is a complex legal system with different laws applying, depending on whether the Commonwealth or a state government is involved.

The Australian dream of owning your own home has become a reality for 72 per cent of Australians aged over 55. By the time we are over 65, 82 per cent of us will own our own home. However, owning even a modest home disqualifies you from legal aid, so most grandparents are not eligible for this type of help. This means that in the event of a custody dispute, the grandparents will have to pay for their legal costs every time there is a hearing, even if the hearing is adjourned. In contrast, their children usually are eligible for legal aid. The grandparents may feel they are in an unequal contest as they can't pursue legal avenues because the costs can become prohibitive. They may feel some degree of injustice about a legal system where they are forced to spend their savings to help their grandchildren while their children are provided with free legal assistance.

Access orders are often made by the Family Court, but when the parents are erratic in exercising their access rights and when they communicate poorly, the grandparents are the ones who are left to cope with the disappointment of the grandchildren who may feel let down yet again.

When Roxanne's parents applied to the Family Court to be given custody of Kelvin, they were pleased that Roxanne didn't contest their application. What they didn't realise was that it is fairly expensive to feed and clothe a growing boy, particularly when it includes school excursions, music lessons and sports uniforms. They were now eligible for Family Tax benefits but, because they had finally paid off their house four years previously, they were ineligible for any of the means tested Centrelink benefits. What was particularly difficult for them was that a year later Roxanne decided she wanted to resume care of Kelvin and with the assistance of legal aid went back to the Family Court. Kelvin's grandparents, being ineligible for legal aid, had to pay all of their own costs including one occasion when Roxanne's illness became particularly difficult and she just didn't turn up for the hearing.

FINANCIAL CONCERNS

It's natural to worry about money, particularly how to make ends meet as the grandchildren become older and more expensive to feed, clothe and educate. A recent survey found that in 34 per cent of grandparent families, one or both grandparents were employed. The remaining two-thirds were self-refunded retirees, worried about how long their funds will last, or grandparents relying on government pensions, allowances or benefits as their main income source. Many people in these situations find themselves spending most of their retirement savings and superannuation on raising their grandchildren.

If the grandchildren have additional health needs, either physical, emotional or intellectual (and a disproportionate number do), the total cost of raising them can be substantial when added to the usual costs of raising children. It's no wonder that some grandparents feel a sense of injustice in being asked to take care of their grandchildren who otherwise would end up in foster care where all of the costs associated with their care, health and education would be met by the government, at considerable expense to the taxpayer. Many grandparents feel that at present they are saving Commonwealth and state governments a lot of money and that they should be treated in the same way as foster parents who look after non-related children. Then they would receive a range of assistance for education, health and living expenses instead of using up their life savings.

COTA National Seniors interviewed a range of grandparents about their experiences in the legal system. Here are three quotes from grandparents who were interviewed:

From a grandmother aged 61 caring for her 10-year-old grand-daughter: 'We've been to court six times. The court gives the mother access but she doesn't exercise it, then 12 months later she turns up demanding to see her daughter. The child doesn't want to go, and anyway, I don't know where the mother lives so I wouldn't let her take the child last time, so now we're going back to court.'

A grandparent couple aged 50 and 54 caring for their two-year-old grandchild: 'Our experience was a positive one. Lawyers were sympathetic and so were the courts. Once the child protection authority could see that we were not neurotic grandparents, they were helpful, however their speed of action was not quick...I find the lack of follow-up advice and interest concerning. No help is forthcoming for advice as to how we could pursue our case.'

Grandparents aged 58 and 63, caring for their 21-month-old grand-daughter: 'Frankly, I am happy about the present situation, however I do worry about the long-term future from time to time.'

There are many agencies you can contact for assistance. These include counselling services such as the relatively recently established Family Relationships Centres. These centres have been set up to be the first port of call when families want information about relationships. They can help with mediation and dispute settlement within the families. They also provide free counselling sessions and can offer telephone information, advice and referral. The Association of Childrens Welfare Agencies can also give advice about where to obtain counselling and assistance if you are finding it difficult to obtain a service.

If you need legal help, general information about the family law may be obtained by calling the Family Law Hotline. This is a free telephone information service for people experiencing family and relationship problems. You could also try the Family Law website set up by the Law Council of Australia.

The Mirabel Foundation is available to assist children who have been orphaned or abandoned due to parental drug use and who are now in the care of extended family. The foundation produces a useful information book *When the Children Arrive*.

General support can be found from Grandparent Support Groups, which provide information on support services for Australians aged over 50 who have taken on the role of parenting. There are grandparents support groups in each state and there are also the more widely known support services such as Anglicare, Centacare, The Smith Family, Barnardos Australia, The Salvation Army and the St Vincent de Paul Society.

Contact details for these organisations can be found in the Appendix.

RELATIONSHIPS WITH THE PARENTS

Despite the awkward situation that has arisen and which has ended in your grandchildren living with you, it is likely that they will have some contact with their parents.

For the children

This situation can be confusing, after all, they are their parents. The normal, ambivalent feelings all children experience towards their parents from time to time are magnified. There may be a mixture of love, anger, wanting to be with them, not wanting to be with them, guilt and worry that it's all their fault, missing the 'freedom' they had with their parents, and being embarrassed about living with their grandparents when nearly all of their friends live with their real parents, and feelings of abandonment and rejection.

As 70 per cent of Australian children living in grandparent families have access to their parents, it's important to try to set up some sort of framework for regular contact and to be able to find common ground on basic child-raising techniques. The last thing you want is for visits to undermine some of the things you have done to improve your grandchild's life. At the same time, you want to avoid undermining and being critical of the child's parents.

You might find it helpful to talk to your grandchildren about how often they would like to see their parents, where they would prefer these meetings to be, whether they want them to be long or short visits and perhaps even if they might like to take a friend. Often when arrangements for visiting are made, children's views aren't taken into account. I'm not suggesting we put them in charge of the visiting program, just that we listen to their views and try to respect their wishes.

There are ways of contact other than face-to-face visits. You may also find it helpful to set up times for regular phone calls as well as making use of email and text messages as other forms of contact for your grandchildren.

For the grandparents

You may feel some of the same emotions as your grandchildren. You may also feel disappointed, let down, angry about the change in your lifestyle, frustrated with your children and perhaps even concerned about the effectiveness of your role as a parent the first time around. Mixed with these emotions will be other times of delight and joy and the new insights which your grandchildren will inevitably bring. You'll still love your children despite all these feelings. You'll see some of their characteristics in your grandchildren. You'll need to work on enhancing the relationship between yourselves and your children as well as your grandchildren and their parents, particularly if there is likely to be any chance of future family reunification.

When you take on the care of your grandchildren you may not know whether it will be a short-term, medium-term or permanent arrangement. After discussing with your grandchildren when, where and how they'd like to see their parents, you can work out a schedule for contact, taking into account the lifestyle of the parents as well.

You might find it helpful to display some photos of the parents on a family photo board. This can include the parents, the parents with their children, you with the parents (that is, you and your children) and you with the grandchildren. You might think this is unrealistic fantasy and in some cases it may be, but where there is a chance of reunification, it's good to work on rebuilding and enhancing all the family relationships.

Remember Esmay and Daryl who were given custody of Liam and his two brothers because of their parents' drug problem? They cared for the three boys for just over two years until Greg and Kelly successfully completed rehabilitation. They are still in the background being supportive, non-judgmental and giving unconditional love as well as practical help when it's needed. They can have the final word: 'Probably the best thing we ever did was take on the care of those three kids. We're not pretending it was easy. It was really tough at times, but to see those boys blossom, develop new skills and return our love has enriched us as much as it has helped them.'

9

Maintaining the Pace

As we've seen in Chapter 1, because people are living longer, some people now have the potential to be grandparents for 50 per cent of their entire life. This means that there will be relatively younger grandparents (like you), somewhat older grandparents and some rather old grandparents. If we are going to keep relating to our grandchildren and if we want them to keep relating to us, we'll need to invest some time in keeping our minds and bodies in good shape.

When our grandchildren are quite young and when we are relatively fit, we can do lots of things with them: get down on the floor to join in their play; play hidings; play chasings; kick balls with them; and take them on outings where we may have to spend half the time running after them. As they become older, so do we. Fortunately, they probably won't be as interested in crawling under the table with us or in setting up a mini-Olympics in the local park, although it may take them a while to realise that our bodies aren't quite as flexible as they used to be and that we can't run quite as fast.

ROLES FOR THE LESS AGILE GRANDPARENT

As we saw in Chapter 4, being a grandparent is an important role and as you become less physically able, that doesn't change. You may no longer be able to take them on a clamber around the rocks at your favourite beach or set up a make-believe camp under the staircase, but the things you can still provide include:

- unconditional love
- being a role model
- security and stability
- keeper of the family history, providing a sense of family continuity
- adviser and counsellor.

OUR MENTAL HEALTH

Have you seen the bumper sticker that says: 'Mental health problems are hereditary. We get them from our children'? Of course that's not true (most of the time) and while most Australian adults enjoy good mental health, almost one in five (18 per cent) have had a mental health disorder at some time during the last 12 months, according to the Australian Bureau of Statistics National Survey on Mental Health and Wellbeing of Adults. That's pretty scary stuff. The good news for us grandparents is that the prevalence of mental health disorders tends to decrease with age. Young adults between 18 and 24 have the highest incidence of mental health disorders (23 per cent) with the level declining steadily with age so that by 65 the prevalence has declined to just over 6 per cent. But that still means one grandparent in 16 will have a mental health problem.

Mental illness can be transient. Some people experience a mental illness only once and fully recover but for others, it might recur throughout their lives.

Although the overall incidence of mental health disorders is similar in men and women, they experience different types of problems. Women are more likely to have anxiety and depressive disorders, while men are more than twice as likely to have substance abuse problems.

Anxiety disorders include conditions which involve feelings of tension, distress and nervousness. People with anxiety disorders may have a constant feeling that something bad is about to happen. They may be perfectionists, often irritable and become upset easily when mistakes are made or if their routine changes. They are sometimes loners or just prefer to hang out with the same, small group of people. They often have a pessimistic outlook on life and may have occasional panic attacks. The highest rate of anxiety disorders occurs in women aged between 45 and 55 (16 per cent).

'I've felt most of those things,' you might say. 'I worry about my children and my grandchildren. I like a routine and I like to do things properly.' Don't worry. That describes most people from time to time. But when some of these thoughts and behaviours start to dominate our lives and become constant features of them, that's the time to seek professional help.

Genevieve had suffered from transient feelings of anxiety and the occasional moment of panic for most of her life, but it was when she became a grandmother for the first time and was asked to mind Jack one day each week, then it became a serious problem. For almost the whole week leading up to Jack's visits she would have difficulty sleeping, and with this being a weekly visit, that meant she had trouble sleeping most nights. She kept worrying that Jack would come down with meningococcal infection while she was minding him (she'd seen a particularly graphic news item on television about this devastating disease) and she kept worrying about baby Jack's future, particularly whether he would become a drug addict, although there was no real basis for this fear.

Her husband became so concerned about her worries that he suggested a visit to the GP. In fact, they went together. The GP diagnosed anxiety disorder and suggested that Genevieve start cognitive behavioural therapy with the help of a clinical psychologist, keeping up his sleeve the option of referral to a psychiatrist should medication be required. He also emphasised the need for regular exercise and healthy eating, gave Genevieve a handout of tips to help with relaxation and suggested to Genevieve's husband that they should talk together about the things that made her anxious.

With the regular help of a clinical psychologist and the support of her husband, along with some modifications to her lifestyle, Genevieve improved considerably. The day each week with Jack became something she started looking forward to and, in response, Jack started to enjoy the visits more as well. He survived childhood without developing meningococcal disease and now, in his early teens, it doesn't look as if he'll turn into a drug addict either.

Depression is more than just feeling a bit low. We all feel sad or moody from time to time, but some people experience these feelings intensely, often for long periods and often for no reason. There are different causes of depression. Sometimes there is a genetic tendency, at other times there is a disturbance in the function of the part of the brain which regulates our mood and sometimes very stressful events or a chain of events can be the cause. Once a health professional has sorted out the underlying cause for the depression, the most appropriate form of treatment can be given.

I was impressed with the story of Li who had emigrated to Australia as a young man, built up a successful business, married an Australian-born girl whose parents had emigrated from the same village as Li's family and was now the very proud grandfather of Patrick. Although Li had been successful in his job as well as his marriage, things didn't seem quite right. He started losing interest in his business, had problems making decisions, had intense feelings of sadness which he couldn't explain and lost his appetite for almost everything except scotch whisky which he started drinking in increasing amounts. Even Patrick, who had gone through the smiling and gurgling stage and was now starting to crawl and squeal with delight when Li visited, failed to cheer him up. When he started to think of suicide he became frightened and asked his family doctor for help.

It was clear that Li was suffering from serious depression. His GP arranged for him to see a psychiatrist. Li felt uncomfortable about this. People in his family just didn't go to psychiatrists. Aren't they for treating mad people? In the end, he reluctantly kept the appointment and was relieved to see that the psychiatrist was a pretty normal person who asked lots of probing questions, but in a sympathetic and understanding way.

The psychiatrist explained to Li that the problem was most likely to do with the strength of the signal being sent between the neurotransmitters in Li's brain (Li wasn't quite sure what this meant, but it sounded convincing) and that in recent years some very effective drugs for treating this type of depression had become available. With medication there was a marked improvement. His appetite improved, most of the time the scotch bottle stayed in the cupboard, he found that he was becoming decisive again and spent every spare moment he could visiting Patrick so that he could get down on the floor to play with him.

Unfortunately, many people with mental health disorders don't seek medical advice. The Australian Bureau of Statistics survey found that only 38 per cent had consulted a health service in the preceding 12 months. That's not very smart when so much good help is available. If you think you or your partner may have a mental health problem make sure that you see a reputable, qualified health professional, preferably on recommendation from your family doctor.

It's important to remember that when people develop a mental illness that it is an actual illness and that is not their fault. Just as we can't totally avoid some infectious diseases, a touch of arthritis, cancer and heart problems, we also can't totally avoid mental illness. But we can do some things to reduce its incidence. Here are some of the things you can do. It's a fairly basic list but there is general agreement that it does help:

- Try to regularly do some things that make you feel worthwhile. Put aside some specific time to relax or to do something which is personal and specifically just for you. Try to do this at lease two or three times each week.
- Be physically active. Exercise helps stimulate the production of hormones, known as endorphins, which help you to feel better about yourself and about your life.
- Have a healthy diet.
- Have a supportive friend or spouse that you can talk to and share feelings with. People who have strong social networks and belong to support groups have more chance of coping with potential mental health problems. Similarly, those with a strong religious faith have a lower incidence of mental health problems.
- Have some regular contact with nature such as gardening, having a pet, walking in the park or along a beach.
- Keep a journal. Many people find that it helps to write down their feelings.

- Try to get enough sleep. You may have to take up some regular exercise to make sure you are tired enough to sleep well.
- Reduce your alcohol intake.

Dementia

Dementia is the term used for a group of diseases which gradually destroy brain cells and lead to a progressive decline in mental function. Alzheimer's disease is the most common cause of dementia. Other causes include conditions which reduce the oxygen supply to the brain, usually from a series of small strokes (vascular dementia), excessive alcohol consumption and a number of rare conditions which all cause a progressive decline in brain function.

None of us want to become demented, but can we do anything to reduce the chance of dementia setting in?

Exercise and dementia

In April 2005 a publication in the *Journal of Neuroscience* showed that mice who exercised regularly had only half of the characteristic brain markers of Alzheimer's disease compared with sedentary mice. These mice also had better reasoning ability in terms of how long it took them to find their way through a maze. 'So what', you say, 'I am a man (or a woman), not a mouse'. The answer is that this finding fits nicely with a Swedish study published six months later in the *Lancet* which showed that people who had participated in physical activity at least twice a week in middle age (the age when people become new grandparents) had a 60 per cent lower risk of Alzheimer's disease than those who had not exercised. This finding added weight to a study published earlier that year which showed that ballroom dancing was associated with a lower risk of dementia. This was thought to be due not just to the physical activity, but also the need to concentrate on complex dance steps and to follow the rhythm of the music.

Isn't it nice to see how one piece of research adds to the accumulating evidence of previous research. Just to complete the picture, in December 2005 a study showed that people who do memory exercises (such as crosswords and Sudoku) as well as physical exercises preserve their memory function as they become older.

Diet and dementia

There is so much written about healthy diets that it's confusing, particularly as much of it is conflicting, sometimes wrong and often based on various opinions of different writers, rather than on any real evidence. Here is a list of foods which can help reduce your chances of developing Alzheimer's disease and will help lower your blood pressure and cholesterol at the same time. The list is based on good scientific studies:

- avocado
- blackcurrants
- curries containing cumin
- dark chocolate
- green tea
- fish eaten three times a week
- olive oil
- red wine (in moderation)
- sage

To consume all of these ingredients at one sitting would be a challenge, but the evidence suggests that incorporating these regularly into the diet can help.

OUR PHYSICAL HEALTH

If we want to live longer and enjoy our grandchildren without being trapped in a body that doesn't work too well, we need to work at it. It won't ever get us back to the level of fitness we had when we were 25. It also won't guarantee to keep us free from disease, although it is known that the risk of developing heart disease, high blood pressure, diabetes and colon cancer are reduced through regular physical activity. There is also a strong link between mind and body so this is also a way that we can help to maintain our mental health.

Being physically active keeps our muscles firmer, our bones hard and our joints more flexible. There are five components of fitness:

cardio-respiratory (aerobic) fitness; muscular endurance; muscular strength; flexibility; and body composition.

1. Cardio-respiratory fitness
   This refers to how effectively the heart can pump blood from the lungs to the muscles during exercise. A healthy heart is one that works effectively and can easily supply the body with blood and oxygen. People who can keep up moderately strenuous exercise over a period of time have good cardio-respiratory (or aerobic) fitness.

2. Muscular endurance
   This is the ability to repeat a movement many times or the ability to hold something in a particular position for a sustained period. Examples would be to pick up your 18-month-old grandchild time and time again because she thinks it's a nice game, or carrying her in your arms for 15 minutes.

...strong link between mind and body

3. Muscular strength

If you had a great deal of muscular strength, you could not only lift your 18-month-old grand-daughter up to see over a crowd, you could also lift your 80-kilogram son-in-law up to see over the crowd, too.

4. Flexibility

Do you remember when you could put your toe in your mouth just like your baby grandson can do now? You were flexible in those days. People with good flexibility can move their joints through a wide range of motion.

5. Body composition

This doesn't refer to what shape you are or how much you weigh. It relates to the proportion of fat, bone and muscle in your body. More of that later.

The benefits of exercise

The benefits of exercise have been known for over 4000 years. In China, it was noticed that individuals who were regularly physically active didn't become ill as often as those who were inactive. This led to the development of kung-fu to help more people exercise on a regular basis and avoid frequent illness. Ancient Persian and Egyptian armies used physical activity and endurance exercises to strengthen soldiers' bodies for warfare.

But is there any need for grandparents to embark on an exercise program even though visits from unruly grandchildren may at times seem like warfare? Don't we have enough to do already? Isn't this mainly for young people? It's surely too late for us. Of course it's not, as many baby boomers and grandparents realise.

Many grandparents spend a fair amount of mental energy thinking about investments for retirement. Which fund? Which shares? Which financial adviser? What type of security will I need? How long will I live? Physical fitness is a cheap investment for retirement. It's likely to prolong your life (a potential problem if your financial investments don't live as long as you do) and reduce illness. Exercise is like a piggy bank. Put something in it on a regular basis and you're likely to save in three areas:

1. fewer medical bills
2. less stress and better emotional health
3. more time.

What's this about more time? Doesn't exercise take time? It does, but fit grandparents move more quickly, have more energy and are more efficient. So you get more things done than when you were only registering 2.4 on the 1 to 10 scale of fitness. Not many retirement advisers suggest including a physical fitness program in the retirement portfolio. Perhaps they should.

You should always be suspicious when one simple thing claims to have so many benefits. Is exercise in the 'snake oil' category? What is the evidence for all these claims about the benefits of exercise and fitness? There is plenty.

Here are some of the benefits of fitness for those aged over 60.

Physical appearance improves

Really? Well, not to the same extent as a weekend with a plastic surgeon, but it certainly helps improve posture and helps us to move more gracefully. Exercise can help straighten up the 'slumping senior'.

Energy increases

Exercise helps relieve fatigue. Having a reasonable level of fitness helps you to do more without feeling as tired.

Confidence increases

People who exercise feel better about themselves. The only downside to this is if we embark on an over-ambitious exercise program, flunk it after a week or two and then feel less fit and less confident than ever. That's why starting slowly, with realistic and achievable goals is important. If you decide to go to a gym, be up front with your instructor on day one. Some are terrific and very understanding but the occasional one will have unrealistic expectations about what your body should be able to do. Tell them that you are not in training for the Commonwealth Games 100-metre hurdles and the shot-put. All you want is a program to improve your muscle tone and cardio-respiratory fitness.

Some seniors find the trim bodies of those portrayed on exercise DVDs to be demoralising because the instructor and all the class participants seem to be so lithe and slim. One grandmother told me that she solved this by shopping around and finding an exercise DVD with an instructor gently teaching a class of middle-aged women of varying shapes. It was a pace she could manage and she felt good exercising in front of the television as she was in better shape than some of those on the screen. However, a regular diet of exercise DVD is pretty boring so she alternated with brisk walks on some days and a few laps at the local pool on other days.

Physical strength improves

As we age, our strength tends to decrease. We won't get back to the strength of our youth but exercise will help to stop the decline and strengthen our muscles, something which will certainly help us to keep up with the grandchildren. Stronger muscles help develop stronger bones and healthier joints. As we build up muscle, we tend to lose fat. We may still weigh the same, but our body composition will improve and we'll look better, too.

Flexibility increases

As we become older, our joints become firmer and our tendons and muscles become tighter. This leads to many of the aches and pains that trouble older people. An exercise program which involves stretching exercises helps our joint mobility and loosens our muscles. This makes muscle injury less likely and improves balance.

Bones become stronger

Toddlers fall over all the time and usually get straight up and back to their activities without any serious damage. It's not quite the same for us mature citizens. Our bones may be thinner and less pliable so that falls may result in broken bones and joint injuries. Exercise improves bone strength, balance and agility. Weight-bearing exercise, such as walking and weight lifting, help to stimulate the formation of bone, thus strengthening our bones and hopefully slowing the development of osteoporosis. This combination of stronger bones, better muscle strength and improved balance helps reduce the risk of falls and the chance of bone injury if a fall does occur.

Tai Chi has been shown to reduce the incidence of falls in older people when compared with those who did not do Tai Chi. The slow, graceful and precise body movements which are required in Tai Chi help to build strength and improve balance, thus reducing the risk of falls. The challenge, of course, is not to fall over while learning Tai Chi.

We get a natural high

After about 20 minutes or longer of exercise, our body releases endorphins. These are related to morphine, but as our own body produces them, they are totally legal. Endorphins act as a pain reliever. They also give a sense of euphoria, so you can get a natural high, just by exercising.

The immune system gets a boost

A healthy immune system helps fight off viral infections such as the common cold and helps build up the body's resistance to a wide range of problems including cancer. It also helps us to recover more quickly from an illness. This doesn't mean that people who exercise regularly won't catch colds or develop cancer, but it does give some protection.

It helps our mind

The exercise–brain connection is real. Exercise helps the mind as well as the body.

You may not be over 65, the age group about to be described, but the time will come when that day arrives. When 174 adults aged over 65 were studied, those who were put into an exercise program involving walking and strengthening exercises had improvement in their memories and had clearer thinking after just 14 days. PET (Positron Emission Tomography) scans even showed that their brains were working more effectively. Just what you need if you have to look after the grandchildren.

The problem with exercise is that it's a bit like spinach. We know it's good for us but we sometimes tend to avoid it. It's not hard to incorporate into your day, however. Why spend five minutes driving round and round a car park looking for a place close to the shopping centre entry when you could park in the empty far corner, walk to the entrance in those five minutes or less and get some extra exercise in the process? Where they are available, use the stairs instead of lifts and escalators.

Barbara was 58 with one grandchild. She and her husband had long been separated. She had a demanding office job, busy but without much exercise, involving working days of 11 to 12 hours with weekends usually spent travelling to see her grand-daughter. Once a year she would treat herself to an interesting holiday and this year she decided to join a group doing the recently opened Great Ocean Road Walk in Victoria. The problem was that she needed to get fit and didn't really have the time to exercise. So she did two things. She parked her car at a different parking lot in the morning which gave her a 15-minute (12 if she stepped it out) walk to the office block and when she arrived, she smiled sweetly at those waiting for the lift and took the stairs to her ninth floor office. Well, that's not exactly what she did. At first she walked one way from the parking lot and took the bus back after work. She gradually increased the number of floors she walked up, first catching the lift to the sixth floor and walking the last three, then walking five floors, then seven and finally nine. It was just over three weeks before she could comfortably walk to and from the car park and up and down nine floors and when she achieved it she felt rather pleased with herself. What she hadn't anticipated was that she seemed to have more energy at work and her ability to solve the newspaper Sudoku puzzle improved. She enjoyed the Great Ocean Road Walk, averaging 14 kilometres a day with the group, made some new friends and then had a few days relaxing and shopping in Melbourne. Even the weather was good. And when she returned home after a break of two weeks, her two-year-old grand-daughter still recognised her.

Ageing and lack of fitness

Many people who were fit in their youth, but not in their fifties and sixties attribute this to the ageing process: 'I could run easily when I was young, but there's no way I could run for a bus now. I'd run out of breath, probably have a heart attack and die.'

This decline in fitness is partly due to the ageing process, but it's related even more to our age group just letting our fitness levels decline. A study published in the highly regarded *American Journal of Cardiology* in 2006 found that when the fitness of 20 to 30 year olds was compared with fitness in 60 to 70 year olds, the younger people were much fitter. Big deal. You don't have to be a scientist to work that out. But what the scientists then did was to put the young and the older subjects through a supervised exercise program for three to six months. They then compared them. The older subjects benefited. They increased their exercise efficiency by 30 per cent. The younger ones improved too, but only by 2 per cent. Why this difference? The older people were a long way behind in fitness at the start of the program and improved so much, largely because they had a lot of leeway to make up. It wasn't so much that they were old, they had just let their fitness levels decline as they became older. The younger people were still fitter, but the difference was now much less after the exercise program. A decrease in fitness is partly a feature of ageing, but it's also a feature of just not keeping fit.

Why bother?

If working on fitness only achieved a little less puff when you have to chase your grandchild, it may not be worth it, especially if you've had to work hard to achieve it. The good news is that you don't have to work very hard. Walking briskly for 25 minutes five times a week (that really just means going out for a 12-and-a-half minute walk, as the other 12-and-a-half minutes happens when you walk home again) significantly reduces the risk of heart disease. So if we build up to that modest goal slowly, do it with a few friends or walk alone listening to your iPod, it's a fairly simple way to ward off heart disease. You'll probably lose a little weight in the process if you don't stop for a meat pie or a thickshake at the 12-and-a-half minute mark.

You may not even need to do as much exercise as that. A study of almost 10,000 adults published in 2004 in the journal *Medicine and Science in Sports and Exercise,* found that people in their fifties and sixties who were regularly active had a 38 per cent lower death rate from a range of conditions: heart disease, diabetes, stroke and even cancer. And they didn't have to be marathon runners. The benefits were shown in those who walked, gardened regularly or even went dancing a few times a week.

Getting started

Okay, I want to be fit, but what can I do? Here are a few simple tips.

Have a check-up

Many people, particularly men, only go to the doctor when they are sick. Why not have a check-up when you are feeling well? Have your blood pressure measured, your urine checked for sugar and protein, a prostate check (for the men), a pap smear and breast check (for the women) along with a general physical examination. Your family doctor can let you know your risk profile for heart disease and can make sure there is nothing which will interfere with you starting an exercise program.

Decide what suits you best

Some people like to walk regularly; some prefer the gym; others a swimming pool. Some prefer ballroom dancing. Ballroom dancing? Yes, dancing is one of the best forms of exercise as it contributes to flexibility, muscular strength and endurance. It also improves body composition and cardiovascular fitness. But of course you have to do it on a regular basis, not just when someone asks you to a ball where, instead of dancing, you stick firmly to your table, eating and drinking in relative safety.

Start slowly

Too many people embark on an exercise regime, overdo it, suffer with aching muscles the next day and give up. As exercise has to be regular and long term to be effective, you don't need to reach your peak performance on the first day. Start slowly and build up gradually, doing a little more every few days.

Exercise with a friend

You might want to exercise alone, which is fine. Others like to exercise with a friend or partner. Apart from the social aspects, a friend can help keep you stay motivated and encourage you to stick to the exercise timetable you've agreed on, particularly on the days when you don't feel like it.

Why not try to have regular exercise with your grandchildren? If they live nearby, you could offer to walk with them to school, or walk home from school. I heard of one grandmother who hated exercise but loved to be with her seven-year-old grandson. So she promised him pocket money if he'd take a short walk with her after school every other day. Both of them thoroughly enjoyed that time together...and her poor circulation gradually improved.

Some infants schools provide the ideal opportunity for walking. Shanti's infants school had organised a 'walking bus' where the parents had made a roster so that they could take it in turns walking to school with a group of children, picking them up as they proceeded to school along the 'bus route'. Shanti's grandmother, Lydia, lived nearby so she joined the roster. This gave her regular exercise where she could be with her grand-daughter, meet some of Shanti's friends and meet some of the other mothers. She also met a couple of other grandmothers once they heard about the idea and decided that they would become 'walking bus drivers' too.

However, it's good for children to understand just what grandparents can do and can't do in terms of physical activity. I almost killed (or at least thought I had) my own grandfather when I was ten. He travelled on the train to visit us and I ran out up to the station, about one-and-a-half kilometres away, to meet him. The problem was me being very keen to get him home. I kept running ahead calling out, 'Hurry up, Grandpa' and 'We have to get home quickly'. Poor Grandpa did his best to keep up a brisk pace but seemed to be very puffed and kept stopping to rest while he wiped his brow. Of course this made me try to hurry him up even more.

When we did arrive home he was bright red in the face, sweating and very short of breath indeed. It took several cups of tea to bring him around. It was only years later that I found he had a serious heart problem which limited his exercise capacity.

Set specific goals

For example, your goal might be a 10-minute brisk walk three days a week for the first week, a 15-minute walk three times in the next week and so on, building up your goal. Or decide how long you'll spend at the gym, or how many laps of the pool you'll complete. Put these dates and times in your diary to record your progress and remind you of your timetable.

Make a list

Write down some of the benefits you expect, but be realistic. You won't lose 25 kilograms and be able to outrun your 12-year-old grand-daughter in the first three weeks, but you should be able to exercise for longer periods than when you started, will probably lose a little weight (although exercise makes you hungry, so be careful what you eat for snacks), and you're likely to sleep more soundly.

Use a pedometer

This will count every step you take during the day. You might only be doing 2000 to 3000 steps per day when you start. Aim for an extra 500 to 1000 steps every few days until you reach around 6000 to 8000 steps per day.

Wear the right shoes

It's worth spending a little extra on shoes that provide good support and cushioning for your feet and other joints. Then you can take every opportunity to exercise.

Finally, a word of advice: if it hurts, don't do it, or do it more gradually and always reward yourself for reaching your goals.

Healthy eating

Our society is obsessed with food and eagerly awaits the next food fad. Magazines are full of articles about how to lose weight, cleanse the body of toxins and eat 'natural foods', whatever that may mean. Before you embark on the Tonsil Cleansing Diet or the Rhubarb Diet (eat three bunches of rhubarb each day and sleep on a pillow made of the rhubarb leaves) or the Cabbage Soup Diet (including a free six-day cabbage detox) it's worth asking if there is any evidence that they work. Why should they work any better than a well-balanced diet, low in fat and with plenty of fruit and vegetables?

Many fad diets do have some elements of truth in them, but these truths are often mixed up with a mixture of bizarre claims clouded in pseudoscientific mumbo jumbo. They sometimes work because to follow them we have to give up a lot of the junk food we've been enjoying. But it's the giving up of the junk food which is the reason for any success, rather than the claims about removing toxins (which our livers and kidneys do perfectly well) or resetting our polarity.

As a grandparent you may want to treat your grandchildren (with their parents' permission, of course) to a fast-food meal occasionally, but don't make a habit of it. You can be a good role model for them if you can all enjoy eating healthy food together.

The food pyramid

The Australian Nutrition Foundation recommends the food pyramid as a good way to remember healthy eating. The base of the pyramid is the 'eat most' section. It includes vegetables, fruits, grains, breads, cereals and nuts. A variety of these foods should be eaten each day.

The middle section of the pyramid is 'eat moderately' and includes fish, lean meat, eggs, skinless chicken, milk, cheese and yoghurt. At least two servings per day of food from this group are recommended.

The top of the pyramid is 'eat in small amounts'. These items include butter, sugar, oils and margarines. A coloured chart displaying the food pyramid can be found at www.nutritionaustralia.org.

I would often be asked to see children because of eating problems. Sometimes they were brought by their grandparents who were minding them on the days when both parents were at work.

The main problems usually revolved around two things. One was a difference in views between what the grandparents expected their grandchildren to eat and what the parents provided for the children and expected them to eat. As you would have already surmised, the grandparents' views tended to be stricter. The other was the age-old concern expressed by parents and grandparents alike: 'He won't eat any vegetables'.

Ron and Kay, the grandparents of young Jordan, came to see me concerned about Jordan's eating pattern, particularly his refusal to eat vegetables. Jordan was delightful, stubborn and somewhat defiant, all pretty normal for a two year old. He was absolutely normal to examine and his weight was right in the middle of the normal range for a boy of his age. When I enquired about his diet it was true that he hardly ate any vegetables but he loved fruit. This was my chance to discuss the food pyramid. Vegetables and fruits are both at the base of the pyramid, the 'eat most' section. It doesn't really matter if two year olds, who regularly eat a variety of fruit, don't eat much in the way of vegetables. When I explained this, as well as pointing out how normally Jordan was growing and developing, Ron and Kay were relieved. They also realised that meals would be more enjoyable if they ceased worrying over the conflict: 'Eat your vegetables, Jordan'... 'I don't like them, Grandma'.

The interesting (but not all that unusual) thing was that the next time I saw them, Jordan had actually started eating broccoli and raw carrot. Once the pressure was off, he found there were actually some vegetables he did like.

The ideal weight and shape

Most of us weigh a little more than we should and that weight seems to be distributed in the wrong places. That's because as we become older, our energy expenditure tends to become less, but our food intake remains much the same, or even increases. Some of us are pear-shaped (wide hips, thick thighs and big bums) and others are apple-shaped, with most of the extra weight around the tummy. It's healthier to be shaped like a pear than an apple. Our fat mostly sits under our skin, on top of our muscle. Apple-shaped people also have a lot of extra fat within their abdominal cavity and around their major organs. It is this intra-abdominal fat which is linked to heart disease and diabetes.

If you read articles about obesity you will notice that the diagnosis of obesity is often based on a person's Body Mass Index (BMI). The BMI is a measure of body weight relative to height. As people become older, BMI becomes less effective as a measure of body fat. A better measure is thought to be the waist-hip ratio (WHR).

This is what you do. Get your tape measure and measure your waist. Resist the temptation to pull the tape measure too tight to get a better reading. Then measure your hip measurement (the widest part of your rear end), near the top of your hip bones. Now measure it again if you forgot to record the numbers the first time and men, remove that bulky wallet which could add a few centimetres to your hip measurement. Get your calculator out and divide the waist measurement by the hip measurement.

Grandmothers, was it 0.8 or less? If so, congratulations, as ideally women should have a WHR of 0.8 or less. Grandfathers, is yours 0.95 or less? If so, congratulations to you, too. And for the majority who have rechecked the measurements, given the calculator a shake to make sure it's working properly and who still exceed 0.8 or 0.95, there are things that can be done about it, things which will improve your health, prolong your life and make you a fitter and more agile grandparent.

Skinny isn't good either

You don't see many anorexic grandparents, but sometimes we eat less than we should, especially if living alone, not feeling well for other reasons or if the decline in our ability to taste and smell makes food less interesting. A study in the UK of almost 15,000 people over 75 years of age found that the really thin ones, particularly the men, had the highest rate of death than in any other weight group. Now I know you won't be 75 for a long time, but this might be a useful piece of information, along with a box of chocolates, to pass on to your own mum and dad, if they are on the very slim side.

Skinny isn't good for grandchildren either. We hear a lot about the obesity epidemic in Australian children and that's a really serious problem, but at the other end of the scale there is a mini epidemic of anorexia, particularly in young girls. At the Children's Hospital we have been seeing girls as young as 10 with severe anorexia. It's not just a condition which makes them look too thin, it can be life-threatening. What can grandparents, particularly grandmothers, do to help?

As you'll remember from your own children, many young teenagers go through a period when they don't want to hear advice from their parents and look to other people to advise them and be their role models. If you have developed a trusting relationship with your grandchildren you'll probably be in a good position to advise them, when they become young teenagers, about the dangers of excessive dieting and the need to have a sensible body shape. They may not be impressed with their parents laying down the law about this, but they just might be receptive to the type of guidance you can give them in this area.

Eating to live longer

Back in 1977, a panel of leading scientists analysed over 4500 research studies from around the world which linked diet with cancer prevention. Their findings are still relevant today. They showed that 30 to 40 per cent of all cases of cancer could be prevented if we did just four things:

1. Eat a healthy diet.
2. Keep physically active.
3. Maintain a healthy body weight, that is not too fat and not too thin.
4. Don't smoke—no tobacco in any form.

We've already covered exercise and body weight. Here are their recommendations for a healthy diet:

- have a diet rich in a variety of plant-based foods
- select foods low in salt and low in fat
- drink alcohol in moderation.

Sounds easy. No special diets, no fads, just a sensible diet, a couple of drinks, a bit of regular walking or other exercise and giving up the fags.

Read the labels

It's worth taking your glasses to the supermarket so that you can read the labels. Some low-fat or fat-free products contain a lot of added sugar, so the calorie level may be high. Be suspicious of some of the claims made by the manufacturers. If the label says '25 per cent less fat', what on earth does that mean? Less than what? And remember that 90 per cent fat-free means 10 per cent fat.

Plant-based foods

Many of us grew up as 'meat and two vegetable' people. But now we know that if we eat more foods that come from plants and less from animals we can reduce our risk of developing cancer and heart disease. It's also easier to reach and maintain a healthier weight. Does that mean no steak, beer and chips? Of course not. It just means that there is more to eating than steak, beer and chips. Have them occasionally by all means, but not as the dietary mainstay.

As a rough guide, work on a quarter of your plate being covered with meat and three-quarters being covered with vegetables.

What's so good about fruit and vegetables? They contain antioxidants and phyto-chemicals (a fancy name for plant chemicals) which reduce the risk of cancer. Antioxidants work by reducing the activity of molecules in the body which damage cells, age tissues and lead to cancer development.

Go for the bright, deep-coloured vegetables. The deeper the colour, the greater the concentration of vitamins, minerals and antioxidants. Dark green vegetables (such as broccoli, spinach and snow peas) and orange ones (kumera, carrot and pumpkin) are good choices.

Meat and fats

A high intake of red meat is associated with an increased risk of cancer of the colon and rectum and probably also the breast and prostate. Limit meat intake to 100 to 150 grams per day and concentrate on lean meats and fish.

Meat contains animal fats which are saturated and not particularly good for our heart and blood vessels, including those blood vessels which supply oxygen to the brain. Like us, animals have much of their fat under the skin, which is why you're supposed to take the skin off cooked chicken before eating it. Fat is also high in calories, so a high-fat diet puts on weight.

Some fat in the diet is essential but some fats are healthier than others. Vegetable oils, such as olive oil and canola oil are best as they are low in saturated fat.

Cakes, pastries, chocolates and the other evil stuff

If you enjoy them (and who doesn't?) don't give them up entirely. Just have them less often and in smaller portions. That way they are more of a treat. They can also be a treat you can share with your grandchildren, particularly if you let your grandchildren see that these really are treats, rather than something which happens all the time. This can be a good lesson for them as they develop their eating habits.

Salt and water

Reducing salt in the diet helps to lower blood pressure. Cut back on salty snacks and processed food. Aim to drink eight glasses of water each day. The time to learn to rely on less salt and to drink water rather than soft drink is in childhood, so you can be an important example here, too. Grandparents who can convince their grandchildren that water is the best way to quench thirst should have their names engraved somewhere and prominently displayed.

Do you need vitamins?

Advertisements will tell you that you do. You don't need extra vitamins nearly as much as you need fruit and vegetables which supply pretty well all of the vitamins we need. Similarly, your grandchildren don't need extra vitamins unless they are medically recommended. The average Australian diet is rich in all the vitamins they need.

See your doctor

When you get your fitness check-up, also let your doctor know about your diet just to make sure that your medications and diet are compatible. For example, grapefruit juice interferes with some blood pressure and cholesterol-lowering drugs.

Grog and smokes

The health risks and benefits of alcohol can be confusing, and that's even if you haven't been drinking. After tobacco, alcohol is the leading cause of drug-related deaths, accounting for over 3000 deaths and over 70,000 admissions to hospital in Australia each year. That's the bad news.

As well as living longer and being healthier to enjoy being a grandparent, we have a real opportunity to be good examples in these areas. I've already said at the end of Chapter 4 that it's not smart to smoke in front of the grandchildren. Your grandchildren look up to you. They'll worship you when they are toddlers and they'll still think you're okay when they are teenagers, particularly as this is the age when they are looking around for role models other than their parents.

So if our main aim in life is to sit down at the end of the day with two or three large drinks or to spend an inordinate amount of time at the pub, that won't go unnoticed by our grandchildren. We have to ask ourselves: Do we want them to turn out the way we would have liked ourselves to have turned out...or do we want them to turn out just like us? It's a sobering (no pun intended) thought and an opportunity to set a good example for our grandchildren.

In 2001, the National Health and Medical Research Council (NHMRC) issued guidelines on alcohol consumption based on how many standard drinks it is safe to consume. Note, this is not the recommended amount to drink. It is the maximum amount which is safe to consume. What is a standard drink? It varies from country to country. In Australia it is 10 grams of pure alcohol. In the USA, where everything is larger, a standard drink is 14 grams of alcohol. So if you follow the NHMRC guidelines when you are in the USA, you'll end up with a nasty hangover.

You don't hear many requests to the barman for '10 grams of pure alcohol please', so here it is in terms we can all understand:

- one can of full-strength beer (375 ml) equals 1.5 standard drinks
- one glass of wine containing 150 ml (the standard restaurant size) equals 1.5 standard drinks
- one nip (30 ml) of spirits equals one standard drink
- one bottle of wine (12.5 per cent alcohol) equals 7.5 standard drinks.

For men, the guidelines suggest an average of no more than four standard drinks a day over a week (up to 28 in a week) and no more than six standard drinks in any one day. For women the recommendation is an average of no more than two standard drinks a day over a week and no more than four in any one day. One or two alcohol-free days each week are recommended.

'All this sounds pretty good', you say, as you head for the wine bottle. But wait, here's the bad news. The body's tolerance for alcohol decreases with age so that older people, that is, grandparents, should consume less than the upper limits described in the NHMRC guidelines.

The good news is that alcohol does have health benefits, but only if taken in moderation. Regular alcohol intake does extend life and reduce the incidence of heart disease, but these benefits are from an intake of one to two standard drinks a day for men and one or less for women. Alcohol consumption beyond this amount confers no extra benefit, it just increases the risk of high blood pressure and stroke. So grandparents who want to live a long life to enjoy their grandchildren as adults and eventually become great-grandparents will benefit from moderate alcohol consumption and alcohol-free days when they are minding their grandchildren.

There is nothing confusing about smoking and health. Tobacco is implicated in 30 per cent of all cancers and contributes to heart disease and stroke. The good news is that, even for a hardened smoker, once smoking is stopped the risk of dying from a smoking-related disease starts to fall.

Five years after stopping smoking, the risk of having a stroke becomes the same as that of a person of the same age who never smoked. Ten years after stopping, the risk of having a heart attack becomes the same as for someone of the same age who never smoked. Even for lung cancer, the risk becomes the same as for a non-smoker 15 years after quitting.

An added benefit is that the grandchildren will stop pestering you for a fag and a light.

10

Giving Your Grandchild Back in One Piece

The last thing you want is an accident when you are looking after your grandchildren. It's not nice for the grandchild and it's not good for your track record as a reliable, highly competent and skilled grandparent. You also don't want to have an accident yourself when you are rushing to snatch your loved one from danger, so we'll have a look at that too.

These days, the child safety experts don't like the term 'accidents' because it implies there is an inevitability about them—that is, 'accidents will happen'—when in fact most accidents, or childhood injuries, can be prevented.

More than half the accidents involving young children occur in and around their home. After all, that's where they spend most of their time. The most dangerous areas of the home are the kitchen and bathroom. Most accidents at home are minor, but still not much fun for the child, or for you. However, a small percentage can be quite serious, leading to severe injury or even death.

Some parts of the house are more dangerous than others. Circulation spaces where people pass each other, such as staircases, or where children like to run and where things may be left lying around to trip over, account for about 20 per cent of home accidents. Many of these are falls.

Around 10 per cent of accidents to children occur in the kitchen. They spend a fair amount of time there to be with their parents, and kitchens are full of dangerous things: boiling water; hot oil; cleaning materials; electrical appliances; knives and other sharp and pointed objects. Scalds are amongst the most common injury that occurs to children in the kitchen area.

The bathroom is another potentially hazardous place, usually because of scalds from hot water, but also from falls in and around the bath or from the pills, razors, scissors and glassware found in the bathroom cupboard.

Home accidents peak at around two years of age. As you'll remember from Chapter 3, children of this age are highly mobile, great climbers, love to test you to see what your reaction will be, have little sense of danger and think they are invincible. So first let's look at accident prevention from a child development point of view and then we'll explore your house and yard looking for hazards.

DIFFERENT DANGERS AT DIFFERENT AGES

Here is some information to refresh your memory about hazards at different ages. In the first two years there are four things to remember:

1. Never underestimate how rapidly a child, especially an infant, develops. Every day the child is developing new skills. Just because potentially dangerous things were 'out of reach' last time your grandchild came to your place, does not mean that they will still be safely out of reach when he next visits.
2. Always be prepared for the unexpected. Your grandchildren will surprise you at the situations they can get into if they aren't carefully supervised. You can check out your house to anticipate and rectify potentially hazardous situations, but there is no substitute for careful supervision. This means no afternoon naps when on duty.
3. Children think differently from adults. Young children have 'magical thinking' and so believe that they have far more power than they actually have. They may think that a

speeding car will get out of their way, or that they can stop it. Like some adults, they believe that the world revolves around them and that they can control it. Accidents occur when they find they can't. Young children are sometimes slow to generalise from one experience to other. They may have learnt that the stove is hot to touch, but still have to learn that the heater is also hot to touch.

4. Children can't always anticipate the consequences of their actions. A swimming pool on a hot day may look tempting enough to jump into, but a young non-swimmer may not realise that the consequences will be to sink to the bottom and stay there.

The first six months

Babies can't really get into danger in their first few months as they are unable to roll until they are four to five months old and they can't do all that much physically. Accidents that occur up to this age are because someone does something to the child, such as giving them the wrong dose of their medicine, dropping them or even deliberately injuring them. Once they start to roll, they are in danger of rolling off the bed or change table unless they are watched constantly. And remember, just because your five-month-old granddaughter can't roll today doesn't mean she won't have developed that skill by tomorrow.

Strollers and prams

A parked stroller or pram, like a parked car, should always have the brake on. You don't want your grandchild to roll away. Also, make sure that the safety-locking device is secure so that the stroller doesn't fold up suddenly.

It is particularly important that parents and grandparents purchase safe products for infants. The Australian Consumers Association, Choice, publishes a book, which is regularly updated called *The Choice Guide to Baby Products* which gives information about what safety features to look for when purchasing items for babies. You can phone Choice on (02) 9577 3399 or go to www.choice.com.au.

Sleeping arrangements

If you are lucky enough to be asked to mind your young grandchild overnight, you'll need safe sleeping arrangements. Don't sleep with a baby in your bed. It may seem like a cute, warm and friendly idea, but there is a real risk of a baby being accidentally smothered when sleeping in the same bed as an adult.

You can use a portable cot or perhaps recycle the one your children used if you can still find it or remember who you lent it to. Just make sure that it complies with current Australian standards (see Chapter 7).

Change tables

When you had your children change tables were a novelty. Now they seem to be standard. You probably don't need one at your place, but if you are babysitting at your children's home, they are likely to have one. The safety rules are the same as for changing a nappy on an ordinary table:

- The table should not be near anything dangerous that the baby can reach.
- Get everything ready first and keep things you need close at hand.
- Never leave the baby on the change table. If you have to turn away, keep one hand on the baby.
- If you have to leave the room, take the baby with you.
- And, of course, it's a great opportunity to talk to your grandchild and have some fun.

Bathing

The reason a baby's skin is so soft and beautiful, compared with ours (sadly), is that it is thin and delicate. This means that it burns easily, from hot water as well as from sunlight. That's why the bathwater must never be too hot. Traditionally (I've no idea why), the temperature is tested with an elbow and if it's comfy for your elbow, it's comfy for the baby.

Don't use much soap. In fact, you don't need to use any. You don't want the baby so soaped up and slippery that she shoots out of your hands.

And never leave the baby, or even toddlers, unattended in the bath for a second. If the telephone rings, ignore it. If the front door bell rings, ignore it. If a fire breaks out in another part of your house, pull the baby out of a bath before you attend to it.

Toys

By six months, the baby can pick up small objects and automatically test them by popping them into the mouth. So toys have to be too large to swallow and too tough to break. Cuddly toys are best at this age, but make sure that the eyes can't be pulled loose.

Car travel

If you can't put your baby grandchild into an approved baby capsule that meets Australian standards, then the baby shouldn't travel in the car at all, even for a quick dash to the shops. You can buy your own capsule, or borrow one, but make sure it is always properly fitted. There is no such thing as a 'little car accident' where children are concerned. Crashing into a stationary object at just 40 kilometres an hour causes the same force to an unrestrained child as falling two storeys onto concrete.

And, of course, it is illegal to leave a child *of any age* alone in a parked car, even if you think it will only be for a moment.

Six to 12 months

This is an age when great strides in development occur. They can sit at around seven months of age, crawl at around nine months, pull themselves up to stand at 10 months and can walk by around 12 to 13 months. By nine months they have developed a pincer grip, which enables them to pick up small objects (pins, dead blowflies, nuts, buttons) that they have crawled towards. Between six and 12 months everything is automatically popped into the mouth, so the nine-month-old has the ability to crawl towards a dangerous object (such as a peanut) deftly pick it up, swiftly pop it into the mouth and perhaps inhale it or choke on it. It's a wonderfully exciting time for the child and for the grandparent who watches these new skills develop but it's also a time when it's good to have anticipated these changes and childproofed your house.

Things that hang down

Beware of things that hang down. Every now and then an infant becomes strangled from playing with a curtain or blind cord, particularly if it hangs near their cot. Just catch up the cords, well out of reach. Remember that the 10 month old likes to pull himself up to stand. You don't want him to do this by pulling on a dangling electric cord, pulling the appliance at the other end down onto his head, or by pulling himself up on a tablecloth, perhaps bringing a scalding cup of coffee onto his face. Similarly, never have a baby on your knee while you are drinking a cup of hot tea or coffee. As part of the curious infant's desire to explore, she may reach out, grab the edge of the cup and tip the contents over herself. Remember, soft, sensitive baby's skin can be badly damaged by hot liquids.

Staircases and ledges

You may have to barricade off some areas of your house so that the young explorer just can't get to them. This is fairly simple when the infant is a visitor, rather than a member of the household. Rooms with doors leading out to decks and ledges should be closed off. If you have a staircase, it's worth investing in a commercial barrier to put at the top or bottom of the staircase. Just remember to take it down after the visit. You don't want to hop out of bed in the middle of the night, crash into the stair barrier and find yourself performing a triple pike and tuck as you dive towards the bottom of the stairs.

Poisons and cleansers

Many tablets look like lollies. All tablets and medicines should be kept out of sight and out of reach, preferably in a medicine cabinet with a childproof lock. As people become older, they tend to have more tablets lying around, often for easy access for themselves. Medications which might help you in the right dose, can kill children.

We sometimes keep medicines and tablets that have been out of date for years 'just in case we need them'. As part of the childproofing procedure, get rid of all your old medications, only keep what's necessary and keep those in a safe place.

Handbags are not safe. They are full of keys, cosmetics, numerous small objects and sometimes tablets. Infants and toddlers love exploring Grandma's handbag, often because they know that Grandma sometimes produces sweet things to eat from it. So never keep pills in your handbag and keep the handbag out of the reach of children. If you're a grandfather who has a handbag, what can I say? Only that it dates you. They went out of fashion years ago.

If you are on some sort of medication (and many of us are as we reach grandparent age), don't take the tablets in front of your grandchildren or you may later discover them trying to do the same thing.

Medicines and tablets aren't the only poisons in the house. Take a good look under the sink. Drain cleaners are particularly dangerous. They are highly caustic, being designed to penetrate through all the gunk which blocks the drain. You don't want that substance to get to work on your grandchildren's mouth or throat. Dishwasher granules and other cleaning materials are also

...never keep pills in your handbag

dangerous. At this age, the toddler becomes expert at opening cupboards but doesn't know how dangerous the cupboard under the sink can be.

As well as removing dangerous objects from kitchen cupboards, for grandfathers who always wanted to indulge in mucking around with pantyhose, here is something you can do. Politely ask your wife (i.e. Grandma) for some old pantyhose. Before she becomes too suspicious, cut them into strips and then tie them into loops which can just connect one toddler height cupboard knob to another. If done well, it will make the cupboard unable to be opened by the toddler, and perhaps even by Grandma.

Toys

Toys should be safe and interesting. Avoid sharp edges and small, detachable parts which the baby will test by popping into his mouth. Electronic toys at this age impress the purchaser more than the baby. Infants like blocks, cardboard boxes and simple toys where sounds can be made and the buttons can be pushed.

Are toys dangerous? Some are. Generally speaking, accidents with toys occur for three main reasons:

1. The toy is used the wrong way: three-year-old Todd throws a toy block at two-year-old Amanda.
2. The toy is unsuitable: skateboards aren't suitable for four year olds.
3. The toy is dangerous: some toys have small, loose parts which can be swallowed or inhaled. Some have sharp edges or rough surfaces and some make such a variety of loud electronic sounds that they drive the grandparents around the twist.

It's worth remembering that toys given to young children aren't always used the way the maker intended. They may be pulled apart, bitten or chewed, thrown about or jumped on. In fact it may end up being you who jumps on that loud, irritating, beeping electronic toy, although it's much more subtle and effective to quietly remove the batteries.

One to two years

Your grandchild is now more mobile and more confident. He becomes good at climbing but does not yet have a well-developed sense of danger. This means that he needs a combination of close supervision and a safe environment. As he approaches two years, he wants to become more independent. He'll test you to see how you react. It's a wonderful age, full of questions, exploration and delight with the occasional bout of frustration. This desire for independence, mixed with a poorly developed sense of danger and a lack of understanding of the consequences of actions, coupled with impulsive behaviour (sounds like a teenager doesn't it) is the reason why toddlers have a high rate of accidents.

Water

Toddlers love water. You and your grandchild can have great fun playing with water: pouring it from one container to another; floating toys in it; making soap bubbles, and just plain splashing. As everyone gets wet you need to dress appropriately as well as having some dry clothes for your grandchild to change into. But *never* leave your grandchild alone near water. This includes baths and ornamental pools as well as swimming pools. Children who drown in swimming pools usually do so in the pool at the house where they are staying. Your own pool is a far greater hazard than your neighbour's pool.

The backyard and garden

You don't want to lose your grandchild, so make sure you have a gate that fastens securely, but don't let this be an excuse for not supervising consistently when outside the house. Have a look around from a child's point of view (yes, try crawling around again, as you did in Chapter 7, or at least bend low). You'll find all sorts of things: ornamental ponds; plants which are poisonous (like oleander, foxglove, angel's trumpet) and plants which may cause a rash in some children (the Robyn Gordon grevillea is a common offender); gardening implements; tools; and an open garage door. Before closing the garage door, take a look inside. What is in there that a toddler can reach and pull down onto himself? What poisons and pesticides are around? Are there any power tools still plugged in? Avoid another sequel to the *Texas Chainsaw Massacre* by making sure that all power tools are switched off and unplugged from the power outlet.

SAFETY ROOM BY ROOM

The kitchen

If you spend a lot of time in the kitchen, your grandchildren will, too. Keep an eye out to make sure that you don't have electric cords dangling over the edge of the countertops, sharp objects in the lower drawers which can easily be reached, and that matches and knives are out of reach. Make sure that saucepan handles don't protrude over the edge of the stove and if the cupboard under the sink contains cleaning agents, drain cleaners, dishwasher powder and other dangerous stuff, preferably move them to a safe place out of sight and reach, or else secure the cupboard with a childproof catch. Similarly, in the laundry don't allow access to bleaches, detergents and other cleaning agents.

Eating and living areas

Avoid tablecloths that can be reached by little fingers and pulled down. Check for unstable TV sets (you'd be surprised how many children have tried to pull themselves up on the TV, only to have it land on top of them), and secure all unstable cupboards and bookcases (those shelves are just the right height for a toddler to climb up). Make sure that heaters have safety covers or that they switch off automatically if toppled over. You also might have to move the coffee table as they are the right height for the toddler to climb onto, with many having sharp corners just at the careering toddler's eye-level. If you have a bar, make sure your grandchild can't get access to the spirits, nuts, corkscrews and wine rack. Wine racks are very convenient if you want to pull out a bottle or two, but if you're a toddler, the bottle you try to pull out might land on your head.

The bathroom

The bathroom is a place where many of us keep potentially hazardous items such as razors, scissors, toilet cleaners, cosmetics (who knows what they put in that stuff?) and glass objects (harmless in themselves, but very nasty once the exploring toddler drops them on the floor). Remember not to leave electrical appliances such as hairdryers or shavers in the power socket, and prevent slipping accidents in the shower and bath by using a skid-proof mat.

A lot of people keep their medications in the bathroom in the hope that when they see their toothbrush and clean their teeth, they'll remember to take their medicine. If you do this, make sure the medications are well out of reach, and preferably out of sight, of your grandchildren, even if the result is that you miss out on cleaning your teeth.

Never leave your grandchild alone in the bathroom. Take her with you when you have to answer the phone (do you really have to answer it?) or if you have to leave the room to some other reason. And don't leave toddlers alone in the bathroom with older children, even if you think it's probably safe.

Garage, toolshed and workshop

These are the places we are always going to 'clean up' or 'clean out' when we have time. The arrival of a grandchild in the family should become the ideal time to put out of reach any sharp tools, solvents, lawnmower fuel, weedkillers, power tools and anything else you can think of. It's a good opportunity to check for any unstable objects which could topple onto the inquisitive young explorer. Having said all that, it's safer to make this area out of bounds to the toddlers anyhow.

WATER AND SWIMMING POOL SAFETY

Australians are great swimmers. Our best swimmers hold multiple records and take home truckloads of medals from the Olympics and Commonwealth Games. But we also have a world record that we don't talk about that much. Australia has more drownings of children under four than any other country in the world. The single most common cause of death in Australian children between one and four years of age is drowning. For every child who drowns there are three children admitted to hospital after a near drowning, with one in eight of these children suffering permanent brain damage.

You thought that the greatest killer of young Australian children was motor vehicle accidents, didn't you? Well, you're almost right. They come a close second. Between five and 15 years of age motor vehicle accidents do become the number one killer, but between one and four years it's drowning.

Why do so many young children drown? They drown because they are attracted to water. They have no fear, are unable to look after themselves in water and drown quickly and silently. They need constant attention when they are near water.

Where do they drown? The commonest place to drown is not the surf, a river or dam. It's the home swimming pool. Would teaching toddlers to swim solve the problem? Not in most cases. It's hard to teach a toddler to swim. Most children aren't able to master swimming until around five years, a good age to learn. They can be taught younger, but it's a lot of work. So now you are asking, 'Well, even if it's a lot of work, isn't it worth it, if you can save a child from drowning?'

It's true that even infants can be taught to roll so that they are face up and float when they are put in deep water. That doesn't mean that they are 'drown proof'. It's one thing for an infant to master this manoeuvre with a parent standing next to him in the water or for a two year old who has been taught the elements of swimming to swim the breadth of the pool towards the encouraging, safe arms of a parent or coach. It's quite another thing for a toddler to fall fully clothed into a pool, when no adult is present, to panic, splash a little, then quietly sink to the bottom. So there you are, my sermon for this chapter, but I've seen too many drowned children not to take this very seriously.

So what can you do if you are a pool owner and your grandchildren come to visit?

Provide constant supervision. This is the most important factor in preventing young children from drowning. A family gathering is a potentially dangerous time as sometimes we each tend to think that someone else is watching the children. It's a good idea to designate one person as the 'water-watcher'. This works at the beach too. The designated person could even wear an armband to indicate their role and must always be at the poolside. A roster system can be worked out to make sure that the poor adult water-watcher isn't totally deprived of fun

Constant supervision and vigilance. I've said it again as it's so important. Get the message?

Above-ground pools are just as dangerous as in-ground pools. Toddlers can even drown in wading pools, so empty them after use.

Pools should be properly fenced. That includes being totally fenced off from the house, with a fence which meets Australian standard 1926, that is, at least 1.2 metres high with no horizontal footholds, the vertical bars no more than 100 millimetres apart (if you are a grandparent over 60, that's 4 inches in the old language) and a self-closing, self-latching gate.

Here are a few other reminders:

- Childproof gates that are propped open are no longer childproof.
- Don't put outdoor tables and chairs up against the pool fence as they make it easier for children to climb the fence which is supposed to keep them out.
- Discourage running around the edges of the pool.
- No glassware should be near the pool.
- Don't be fooled into thinking that a non-swimmer will be safe with a flotation device.
- Keep a resuscitation chart clearly displayed in the pool area.
- Learn cardio-pulmonary resuscitation. CPR courses in basic resuscitation are available from the Royal Life Saving Society, the Red Cross and St John Ambulance. See Chapter 11 and the Appendix at the end of this book.
- Don't put too much trust in pool alarms or pool covers.
- Store pool chemicals in dry areas, well out of the reach of children.
- Provide constant supervision.

Sunburn

Most of us are aware of the hazards of sunburn, not just the immediate discomfort, but also the long-term damage to the skin, including the increased risk of skin cancer. In fact, we occasionally go over the top to the degree that some children who are protected almost totally from the sun are starting to develop rickets. Sunlight is good. It helps children to make vitamin D, which builds strong bones. It's a matter of getting the right balance, enough for healthy growth and not enough to cause skin damage.

I can't help having a quiet chuckle at the beach when dad appears in a budgie-smuggler, mum in a brief, fetching one-piece item and the children are almost totally covered in sun protection swimwear. Of course sun protection for children is important, especially in the hottest part of the day, but the incongruity between the parents' and the children's swimwear is intriguing.

Hats are important, with all-round brims much better than caps. And, of course, use SPF 30 sunscreen. If you purchase sun protection products from Cancer Council stores, the profits help to fund cancer research.

CAR AND DRIVEWAY SAFETY

It's a sad fact, but every year children are run over by people who love and care for them. The driver doesn't mean to do it and they don't even see it happening. It happens in their own driveway. It's hard to see a small child in the driveway as you reverse.

Have you noticed how your neck doesn't swivel as well as it did when you were in your twenties? That makes it even more difficult to see what's behind you. Studies have shown that, even when using rear vision mirrors, there is more than a 'blind spot' behind a car: it's a 'blind space'.

It only takes a few moments for a young child to move from the safe place, where you saw him a moment ago as you went into the car, into the driveway, right behind your car.

Here's what to do to avoid running over your grandchild in the driveway:

- Think of the driveway as a road. It's best not used as a play area.
- When you go to drive away, make sure the child is supervised by another adult, preferably within the house.
- If you're the only adult at home and need to move your car (but do you really need to move it?), even if only a few metres, take your grandchild with you. That means placing him securely in the car in a suitable child seat restraint.

Car doors and traffic

It's no fun trying to get a child out of a car parked on a busy road if you have to do it from the road side, rather than the kerb side. The smart thing is to put your grandchild's infant car seat in the rear seat behind the front passenger seat. That makes it easier for you both to chat as you drive along, (but no eye-contact please) and means that you can get them out from the kerb side. If you have two or more grandchildren, get them out one by one on the kerb side, starting with the eldest and have them hold hands and touch the side of the car while waiting for you to finish.

Seat restraint

You will have to invest in child safety seats if you are going to be driving your grandchildren. If you don't, and if you can't borrow some, you won't be able to drive them around. Child safety restraints and seats have improved considerably since we were young parents. Some parents are happy to let their new baby travel in the old folks' car, but don't be surprised if they aren't, so it's best to sort this out before investing in an infant restraint. If you can afford it, buy an appropriate child seat for them as a gift. They'll have to have one and they just might let you borrow it, along with their baby.

There are different requirements for different ages:

1. **Birth to six months**: A rear-facing baby capsule (for babies up to 9 kilograms) is required. This is kept in place by the car seatbelt and the capsule's tethering strap.

2. **Six months to four years:** Forward-facing seat (for children 8 to 18 kilograms) held in place by the car seatbelt and the baby seat's tethering strap. The child is buckled into the seat with a five-point harness. Some are easier to do up than others. If your grandchild is a wriggler, you may have to have some practice first. There is also a convertible restraint seat suitable from birth to four years (or 18 kilograms), which is initially used in a rear-facing format and can then be converted to a forward-facing seat as the child grows larger.

3. **Children older than four years:** A booster seat (for children greater than 18 kilograms) which elevates the child so that the car's lap/sash seatbelt can be used. However, make sure that the sash is on your grandchild's shoulder, not the neck.

If in doubt, call the Child Restraint Information Line on 1800 802 244.

Hot car warning

None of us would be silly enough to leave our grandchild in the seat restraint while we slipped out of the car for 'just a moment' to collect something, or to run back inside to answer the phone. But just in case you will ever be tempted to do this, there are two things to remember:

1. 'Just a moment' may stretch into a few minutes or longer.
2. On an average Australian summer day the temperature inside a parked car can be 30 to 40 degrees *higher* than the outside temperature. That's right, 30 to 40 degrees. That means that if it's 30°C outside, the interior of a car could be 70°C. This is a good temperature for slow baking Atlantic salmon, but a potentially lethal one for a child. Even having the windows open 5 centimetres to let just a little air in doesn't help much. Experiments have shown that the inside of a car with the windows up can reach 78°C on a hot day, but even with the windows opened a little, the temperature can still rise to 70°C.

OTHER HAZARDS

This list might make your home look too dangerous even for you to live in. It's not, of course, but paying attention to some of these things, such as electrical safety, glass doors and scatter rugs, may also save you from having an accident:

- electric sockets. Put child-resistant covers over electrical outlets. If you haven't had a circuit breaker installed, this would be a good time to do it
- glass doors and large windows. To avoid running into or through a glass door, put small stickers on it, at child eye-level as well as at adult eye-level
- scatter rugs on polished floors. Get rid of them or use a non-slip underlay cut to the size of the rug
- plastic bags. These are a suffocation hazard. Tie a knot in them before storing
- furniture. Furniture needs to be stable so that it is unable to be tipped over when a young adventurer attempts to climb it. Rearrange furniture to avoid collisions with hard corners
- heaters should not be too hot to touch and should have a safety cut-out feature which turns the heater off if it tips over. Don't leave them on all night in your grandchildren's room when they stay overnight. You can turn it on to warm the room and turn it off when they are put to bed
- smoke alarms. This isn't a hazard, but it's a good time to remember to install some if you don't already have them
- pets. It's heresy, I know, but small children and dogs can be a risky combination. If your grandchild is visiting and you have a dog, there are a few simple rules. Don't let them disturb the dog when he is asleep. Don't let them tease or over-excite the dog. Don't let them take his food. Don't let your grandchild's face get too close to the dog's mouth (many dog bites to children occur on the face, just because the child gets his face too close to the dog when the dog is excited or eating). Other pets (apart from child unfriendly ones such as snakes,

funnel-webs and ferrets) are okay and are probably more likely to become injured by the child than vice versa.

- hot water. Each year, more than a thousand children are admitted to Australian hospitals because of scalds. Most scalds are caused by tap water which is just too hot, with most of these scalds occurring in the bathroom. Sometimes they can occur when a child is plunged into the bath before the water temperature is checked. At other times, bathroom scalds occur when an unsupervised child turns on the hot tap. Many home hot water systems deliver water between 65 and 75°C. This is a problem, as at 60°C, water can cause a full thickness (third-degree) burn in less than one second. At 50°C it takes five minutes to cause a full thickness burn, so a system that mixes hot and cold water to reduce the delivery temperature, particularly the bathroom, will prevent a lot of scalds. Australian Standards recommends 50°C as the maximum hot water delivery temperature for the bathroom.

Children and grandparents have more in common than a delight in each other's company. As I've already mentioned, children, particularly babies and toddlers, have softer, more delicate skin than adults, which is why hot water and sunburn are more hazardous in these years. Sadly, as we get into later years, our skin becomes thin and more delicate, too (it's just not as cute) and the risk of damage from hot water increases. As a valuable safety measure, you might want to consider paying to have a tempering valve or a thermostatic mixer installed as a gift in your children's home, if they don't already have one. If you don't have some form of temperature control system in your own bathroom, remember to always turn the cold water on first and turn it off last when running the bath.

An excellent resource about child safety is Kidsafe (The Child Accident Prevention Foundation of Australia) www.kidsafe.com.au. See the Appendix for more safety information.

11

Emergencies and First Aid

Y ou're minding your grandchild, possibly as a much-anticipated sleepover. Everything is going well, but then she develops a high fever and a blotchy rash or perhaps becomes short of breath and starts to wheeze. What can you do? As one of the characters says in the *Hitchhiker's Guide to the Galaxy* (perhaps it was Zaphod Beeblebrox, or maybe some other character with an equally improbable name), 'Don't panic'.

COMMON EMERGENCIES

Don't panic, but do take action. This chapter isn't a medical textbook, or a comprehensive guide on all the emergencies you might encounter, but an outline, in alphabetical order, of a few common emergencies with some advice about what to do.

Allergic reactions

Your four-year-old grand-daughter, Emily, is staying at your place. During the day you notice that she has developed a red, raised, itchy rash on her face and body. She also looks slightly puffy around the eyes but she is still full of energy and playing happily as usual. It's probably an allergic reaction. Up to 40 per cent of children will have an allergic reaction at some time or other. Most are mild, but occasionally an allergic reaction can be severe and life-threatening. This is when you need to call an ambulance immediately. In a severe allergic reaction (called an anaphylactic reaction) the child becomes red and flushed, then pale, develops a rash, often some facial swelling and may develop a hoarse voice and have difficulty breathing. This is an emergency. Call 000.

Bangs, bruises and swellings

A bang or a sharp bump will often lead to swelling and may bruise. You don't want to return your five-year-old grandson looking as if he's done a few rounds with Anthony Mundine, so here's what you do:

Apply a cold compress (see page 200) to reduce swelling and then rest the injured area. If the injury is to an arm or leg, raising it (such as resting it on a cushion or pillow) will help to reduce swelling. This won't make much difference to any bruising (bruising occurs when tiny blood vessels break and blood leaks out under the skin), but at least you'll feel you've done something to help and your grandchild will enjoy the sympathy.

Blisters

Blisters occur when an area of skin is burned, or from repeated friction to a small area. They can also sometimes occur from insect bites. It's wise not to puncture them or cut off their tops as this increases the chance of a blister becoming infected. Blisters heal best if exposed to the air, so all you need to do is clean the surrounding area and if the blister is raw or broken, apply an adhesive strip.

Choking

See **Swallowed objects and choking**

Convulsions, fits and seizures

These are just three different words for basically the same thing. Convulsions are produced by a sudden increase in the brain's electrical activity. The most common things to trigger a convulsion are a high fever in children under six years (this is commonly known as a febrile convulsion and is the commonest type of convulsion), a head injury or an infection involving the brain. However, often no cause is found. Most convulsions last for less than five minutes. Epilepsy refers to a tendency to have convulsions, which are not caused by a fever.

Although the child is unconscious during a convulsion and does not suffer, it can be terrifying for the parent or grandparent seeing one for the first time. I would often take medical students to see a child who had come to hospital with a febrile convulsion. The young child would be happily playing in bed, with Mum and Dad ready to take him home. I'd get one of the students to ask the parent, 'What was going through your mind when he had the convulsion?'

The reply was always the same: 'I thought he was going to die'.

Of course, he wasn't going to die and was now quite well, but this little exercise was done to help the students see things from the parents' point of view and to realise just how frightening it is to see your child having a convulsion. So if none of your children have ever had a convulsion and if one of your grandchildren has one when you are minding them, you'll probably experience the same terrifying emotion.

It's always good to have the doctor check out a child who has had a convulsion, even though your grandchild might seem fine afterwards. You should call an ambulance if the convulsion lasts for more than five minutes; if there is more than one convulsion; or if the child has trouble breathing and looks unwell as these things may mean that medical intervention is required.

You'll probably want to mention all this to the parents as well.

Cuts and grazes

These are another hazard of childhood, particularly grazed knees. The first thing to do, after giving your child a cuddle, is to remove any particles of dirt and to wash the area gently with a gauze pad or soft cloth. Don't use a face washer, which is too rough. There is no real need for antiseptic solutions, just soap and water work fine.

Grazes heal more quickly if they are left open. If they are covered with a dressing, they tend to remain moist and heal more slowly.

If the injury is a cut, and if it is bleeding heavily, apply pressure with a clean pad. Hold it firmly in place for at least five minutes. This will usually be enough to stop the bleeding. Deep cuts, of course, require medical attention.

Diarrhoea and vomiting

You'll probably be worried that this is due to your grandchild's dislike of your cooking, but you can always blame it on that takeaway meal they talked you into. In fact, most gastroenteritis is caused by a virus infection and usually has little to do with food and cooking. The main concern in children is loss of too much fluid from diarrhoea and vomiting, leading to dehydration.

Medicines and diarrhoea mixtures are of little use and sometimes cause problems of their own. The secret of managing diarrhoea is to give small amounts of fluids frequently. Oral rehydration fluids, available from pharmacies are best, but you could make do with diluted fruit juice or diluted lemonade (four parts of water to one part juice or lemonade).

Diarrhoea tends to be infectious. To stop it spreading from little Alfred to his sisters Jemima and Kahlia, to yourself and then on to Mum and Dad when the children return home, be very strict about everybody washing hands after using the toilet.

As gastroenteritis can be potentially serious, especially in young children, or if the diarrhoea and vomiting is not due to gastroenteritis at all, but rather to some other problem, the warnings that medical help is needed include: blood in the stool; persistent abdominal pain; persisting temperature over 38°C; inability to keep any fluids down; drowsiness; and less urine being passed than usual.

'He's drinking but he hasn't eaten anything all day,' you say. 'Surely this can't be good for him? Children need food to grow. Will he become malnourished?'

As we've already noted, grandparents, as well as parents, worry if their children don't eat enough. But if you're not feeling good, you often don't want to eat, particularly if the illness involves nausea and vomiting, or if you have a sore throat. Don't worry. No child has ever starved to death or become malnourished in just a couple of days. We notice and worry when they don't eat, what we tend to overlook is how quickly they make up for it as soon as they are well.

Fever

The normal body temperature is 37°C with a normal variation of 0.5°C either way. This means a fever is a temperature above 37.5°C.

Fever is the way the body responds to fight off infection. Most infections are caused by viruses, so antibiotics don't make any difference although occasionally the infection will be due to bacteria, which may result in a serious illness if not treated properly. If your grandchild has any of the following, seek medical help:

- seems very unwell
- has a rash
- has a stiff neck
- is drowsy
- has trouble swallowing
- is breathing rapidly
- has an earache.

If none of these symptoms are present, the following simple measures will suffice.

Take off any warm clothes and don't wrap your grandchild up in blankets. That old-fashioned story about 'sweating it out' is a furphy and can even be dangerous. Offer plenty of fluids and don't worry if they don't want to eat. To lower the temperature and to make your grandchild feel more comfortable, you can sponge them in lukewarm water and give paracetamol or ibuprofen, strictly as directed on the bottle. Aspirin is not safe for children under 12 years of age.

A fever in a child can have different causes. Sometimes it's a minor problem and at other times it can be quite serious, particularly in infants and babies.

Four-year-old Helen was spending the day with her grandparents, Gwen and Bruce. Just after lunch, Gwen noticed that Helen looked a little flushed, felt warm and had a runny nose. Gwen took her temperature, which was 38.5°C. There were no spots or rashes on Helen's body and she was playing quite happily, although she hadn't eaten as much lunch as usual. Gwen remembered that Helen's older brother had a nasty cold late last week and had to miss a couple of days from school. She thought that Helen was probably coming down with the same infection. Gwen didn't fuss too much, didn't bother about Helen not eating all of her lunch and just kept a quiet eye on her, giving her plenty to drink. Bruce wasn't much good at this sort of thing but did his bit by reading Helen an action story in which she participated with gusto. Helen was much the same when her parents collected her and over the next day it became obvious that her brother's cold had now become Helen's cold.

Nathan was just eight months old. His parents hadn't left him before, but when his father, Chris, won the office raffle first prize of a dinner for two at a swank city hotel, they decided to make the break and asked Megan's parents to babysit. Megan and Chris left looking resplendent, after first giving Megan's parents so many instructions about Nathan that it almost made them wonder how they had ever managed to rear their own children successfully. Nathan seemed unfazed by all the fuss, took his bottle happily (he'd been weaned a month ago) and settled down to sleep.

Just before 9 pm he woke crying. Megan's mother noticed that he felt hot and when she turned on the light in his room she noticed that he seemed to be breathing more rapidly than usual and didn't look quite as bright-eyed and alert as he normally did. She offered him his bottle but he wasn't interested, something which was unusual for Nathan, as the family often joked that he'd be happy to have a drink anytime. Megan's mother had a strong feeling that things weren't right. She called Megan's mobile to tell her that Nathan wasn't well and that she was about to take him to the nearest hospital emergency department where they could meet. At the hospital it was clear that Nathan was becoming more unwell by the minute. Tests were quickly done and he was started on intravenous antibiotics for a suspected infection in the bloodstream, a diagnosis which turned out to be correct. He made an uneventful recovery from this serious infection, but only because prompt treatment had commenced.

These two stories show how a fever in a child can mean different things at different times. In Nathan's case, what if the hospital had found nothing wrong? Did Megan's mother over-react? No, she trusted her instincts and combined this with the knowledge that a very young child with a fever, rapid breathing, no interest in feeding and a lethargic look could be cooking up a serious infection. And even if nothing was found to be wrong with Nathan, she still took the wise course, as you never can tell. What about Helen's grandparents? Were they too laid back? Should they have seen a doctor? Helen was bright-eyed, alert and was playing enthusiastically but to be sure, her grandmother sensibly kept a watchful eye on things 'just in case'.

Fits
See **Convulsions, fits and seizures**

Head injury
Most head injuries are minor. You hear a thud, think the worst, your grandchild cries briefly, perhaps wants a cuddle and then returns to what he was doing before. In these cases you don't have to do anything apart from a little comforting if that is needed.

The things which should make you seek prompt medical assessment and help after a head injury include your grandchild becoming drowsy or losing consciousness (you don't really need a book to convince you of that one); a headache that is severe and persistent; vomiting; any bleeding from the ear; or if your grandchild becomes clumsy, confused, disoriented, has memory loss or has a convulsion.

Insect stings and mozzie bites
You've taken Joshua and Phoebe on an outing to the park. It's spring, the clover is in bloom, your grandchildren are playing amongst it when suddenly Joshua screams. You wonder to your horror if he's been bitten by a snake as you rush over to find a bee sting protruding from his finger.

Insect stings need to be removed. If you try to pull them out, they are likely to be squeezed in the process and more poison will go into the wound. Scraping a fingernail across the sting or sliding a credit card across it (all credit cards are accepted) will usually remove it. Apply a cold compress (see page 200) as soon as you can as this will reduce pain and swelling.

Mosquito bites cause swelling in some children and not in others. If your grandchild is one of the swelling variety, the bite will swell less if a cold compress is used. Itching can be relieved with calamine lotion or an antihistamine cream. It's worth doing this as scratched bites may become infected.

When ticks bite, they bury their head and jaws beneath the skin with their body protruding. Try to pull the tick out in one piece, using tweezers. Some people suggest putting a little kerosene or mineral turpentine on the tick first to make it loosen its grip. If you decide to use kerosene or turps, remember that they are poisonous to children as well as to ticks, so put the lid back on firmly and place the container out of reach.

Tick paralysis is rare, but if your grandchild develops any unsteadiness, double vision or difficulty breathing or swallowing, see your doctor quickly.

Meningococcal infection

Everybody seems to know about meningococcal infection and everybody dreads it. And rightly so, too, because it can be a rapidly progressing, devastating infection. The good news is that despite the publicity, meningococcal is a fairly rare condition. But it is very dangerous. Prompt treatment in hospital with intravenous antibiotics and fluids usually leads to complete recovery, but early diagnosis is essential. Seek quick medical help if there are any of these symptoms: a rash, typically purple, sometimes with smaller spots, and often spreading and becoming blotchy; fever and drowsiness; convulsions.

Rashes are common in children, so how can you tell if the rash is a sign of meningococcal disease? Just press a clear-coloured glass firmly against the rash. In most rashes, the skin under the glass goes white and the rash disappears while the glass is being held firmly against the skin. If the rash doesn't fade when you do this, it may be a meningococcal rash.

Nosebleeds

You are minding five-year-old Laura. Everything is going well until she runs up to you with blood trickling from her nose and running over her top lip. She hasn't had an injury, but her nose seems to have started bleeding spontaneously.

Lots of nonsense has been written and passed on by friends and families about how to treat nosebleeds. Forget about ice packs to the forehead, and cold keys to the back of the neck. Bleeding almost always comes from inside the lower part of the nostril, sometimes when the child picks her nose, sometimes when the nose is congested from a cold and when there is lots of nose blowing, but usually it just comes out of the blue.

All you have to do is sit your grandchild down, leaning forward (preferably not on your white carpet) and hold the bottom (fleshy) part of her nose firmly between your finger and thumb for at least 5 minutes, preferably ten.

After two minutes it will seem like you have been doing it for 10 minutes already, so do it by the clock. It's really important that you grip the bottom part of the nose. Holding the top (the bit which you can't wobble and where you can feel the nose bone under your fingers) won't achieve anything.

If any blood has run back into her mouth, just get her to spit it out, again avoiding your carpet. Disturbing the nostril may restart the bleeding so (easier said than done) tell her not to blow her nose or pick it for as long as possible after the bleeding stops.

If the bleeding does start again, go through the same process, pinching the nose for another 10 minutes.

Poisoning

Little Laura's nose has now stopped bleeding with your help and she is playing quietly while you clean up. When you check her, you noticed that she has found some tablets. They are scattered on the floor, she is holding a couple and one is in her mouth. She may have swallowed many already. What do you do? Don't panic. Telephone the Poisons Information Centre from anywhere in Australia 24 hours a day on 13 11 26. Tell them what the swallowed tablet or substance is and follow their advice. If that advice includes taking your child to a hospital emergency department, bring the container and any remaining contents with you.

Scalds

Even after all the precautions in the previous chapter (you did read that one, didn't you?) a cup of recently poured tea is knocked over and scalds your grandchild. Don't panic. Act quickly, *very quickly*. The first thing to do is remove all wet clothing from the child as it's hot and will continue to burn the skin. If some has spilled on you, remove your wet clothes too, but do your grandchild's first. Then run cold water over the burn for 30 minutes. Yes 30 minutes, despite any water-saving restrictions there may be. This will prevent the burn from going deeper into the skin.

Do not apply ice, butter, margarine, oil, soy sauce, tofu, toothpaste or any other folk remedy you may have heard about. While you are wasting time looking for the butter, and wondering whether unsalted butter may be better, the burn will be penetrating deeper into the skin. Just use cold water, lots of it and, most important, do it immediately.

If the burn involves your grandchild's face or hands, if it blisters or if it's larger in area than the size of the child's palm, seek medical help, but only after 30 minutes of cold water treatment.

Splinters

Splinters don't seem as common as they used to, perhaps because children aren't out in the backyard as much playing with sticks and blocks of wood. But when they do occur they hurt, have the potential to introduce infection and so need to be removed. First, clean the area gently with soap and water, then pass some tweezers over a burning match for a few seconds to sterilise them and let them cool. Next, with lots of encouragement for your grandchild to hold still (and preferably with the other grandparent to both hold and comfort) pull the splinter out with the tweezers, pulling at the same angle by which the splinter entered. Next, squeeze the area gently. This may make it bleed slightly but this is good as it will flush out any dirt. Now wash the area again and cover with an adhesive strip. The adhesive strip isn't really necessary, but children like them.

Sprains

A sprained ankle is the commonest sprain in children. They'll cry out, limp and the ankle will start to swell. The first thing to do is remove the shoe and sock and then apply a cold compress (see page 200) to reduce swelling. You can then bandage the ankle and keep it elevated. The bandage should be firm, but not too tight to be uncomfortable as this may mean it is interfering with the circulation. If the swelling is marked, or if pain is severe, there may be a fracture so you should see a doctor for an examination and possibly an X-ray.

Swallowed objects and choking

Back in the days when we had one- and two-cent coins, I saw a child whose parents had brought him to the Children's Hospital Emergency Department because he had swallowed two cents. An X-ray probably wasn't necessary, but as the child was only 16 months old, I did one to make sure that the coin hadn't become stuck in the oesophagus and that it was now in the stomach and safely on its way out. When I looked at the X-ray, I realised that the parents were absolutely right. There in the stomach were two separate objects, each a one-cent coin. He had indeed 'swallowed two cents'.

It's amazing what a young child will swallow. Favourite objects are buttons, coins, fruit seeds, eyes pulled off soft toys and wheels pulled off small cars. Fortunately, these things and even sharp objects such as pins and pieces of glass, pass through the bowel with the greatest of ease. So if your grandchild seems well and continues to be well, you don't have to do much except tell the parents. This saves them becoming anxious a couple of days later when they change a nappy and find an eye staring back at them out of the poo. In most cases, swallowed objects are likely to cause more stress and anxiety to us than to our grandchildren.

One exception is those small, round batteries, such as those used in watches and some toys. These can be corrosive and medical advice is needed.

If a child swallows something that can dissolve, this can be potentially serious, possibly leading to poisoning. Call the Poisons Information Centre on 13 11 26 for advice.

Choking is a different matter. In choking, the small object doesn't go into the stomach, but instead is lodged in the windpipe. If the child is still able to breathe comfortably, seek immediate medical help. Attempting to dislodge an object that is partly obstructing breathing may lead to complete obstruction.

If the child can't breathe, act immediately. If under 12 months, hold the baby head down on your thigh or lap and with the heel of your other hand give five firm blows to the middle of the back, just below the shoulderblades.

For children over 12 months, put the child in front of you and put your arms around him so that your fist is just below his breastbone. Put your other hand on the fist and thrust both hands sharply upwards. Do this several times until the object is expelled.

Wheezing and shortness of breath

When a child's lower breathing tubes (bronchi and bronchioles) become narrowed, the air flowing through them as the child breathes makes a high-pitched, whistling sound. The child may also breathe more quickly and seem to have to work a little to get air in and out. This is 'shortness of breath' and the sound is referred to as wheezing. The commonest cause is asthma.

Sometimes a foreign body (such as a peanut) may become inhaled and lodge in one of the airways, causing wheezing. Sometimes wheezing occurs with respiratory infections. The importance of wheezing is that it is a sign of difficulty in breathing. If you know that your grandchild has asthma, you'll need to have his asthma medication and a copy of his asthma management plan with you whenever you mind him. If he starts to wheeze, asthma is the most likely cause, so give him his asthma medication in the correct dosage, according to his asthma management plan. As well as telling you what to do as soon as wheezing occurs, the asthma management plan will outline the steps to take if the wheezing doesn't respond, right through to advising you when to seek medical help. An up-to-date asthma management plan makes a big difference to treating asthma, ensuring that early treatment is provided so that the asthma episode can respond quickly. It also gives parents, grandparents and older children (who can learn to manage their own asthma), a sense of confidence and control.

SIMPLE FIRST AID

It's a good idea to have at least two first-aid kits, then one can be kept in the car, but remember where you have put the one that you keep at home. You can purchase a first-aid kit from a pharmacy or make your own. If you make your own, include:

- some bandages: a small and a large roller bandage; a small and a large compression bandage; a triangular bandage for making a sling and a finger bandage
- some dressings: non-stick ones in several sizes, some gauze swabs and some sterile eye pads
- adhesive strips in different shapes and sizes
- sticking tape (buy the hypo-allergenic variety) to hold dressings in place
- scissors
- tweezers
- safety pins
- disposable gloves
- thermometer.

Some of the more common items you'll probably use are listed below.

Bandages

Their uses include:

- to make the child with a minor injury feel important
- to help support injuries; for example, a sling to elevate a sprained wrist
- controlling bleeding
- holding dressings in place.

...to make the child with a minor injury feel important

They need to be secure enough to do their job but not applied so tightly that they cause discomfort and interfere with circulation.

A cold compress

This is good for reducing swelling and pain. You can make one by:

- rinsing a facecloth in cold water, ringing it out and putting it on the injury. You need to keep it cool by repeating this step every five minutes or so
- wrapping a pack of frozen peas (even if your grandchild hates peas) in a thin towel and applying it to the injury. Other frozen items will do as long as there is enough movement in them to cover the injured area
- half filling a plastic bag with ice blocks and a small amount of water, sealing the end, wrapping it in a thin towel and applying it to the painful or swollen area.

Dressings

Dressings keep wounds clean and help to prevent infection. Cotton wool (even though we may have used it on our children and our parents used it on us) is out. All those fluffy bits just stick to the wound. Gauze pads are best, especially if they are of the non-stick variety or impregnated with petroleum jelly.

Small cuts only need an adhesive strip. They are very effective for stopping crying when there has been a minor injury. It's worth keeping some handy, particularly ones featuring cartoon characters.

A WORD ABOUT CRYING

You are minding your grandchildren and five-year-old Jonah falls on the footpath and grazes his knee. It hurts (grazes often hurt more than cuts since, because of their size, they irritate a much larger number of pain nerve endings near the surface of the skin). Jonah cries loudly. Grandpa, who is from the 'I did it tough when I was a child and it didn't hurt me' school, says, 'Stop crying, it's not hurting'. Jonah now cries even more loudly. Grandma then calls Jonah over, saying, 'Here, let me have a look. I bet that's sore. Let's clean it up to get rid of any germs.' Jonah stops crying and is soon back playing happily.

When we injure ourselves, it hurts. When children fall over and injure themselves, it hurts too. They normally cry and want a little sympathy. Excessive sympathy and rewards for minor injuries is not a good idea as it is likely to promote 'sick behaviour'. On the other hand, it just doesn't make sense, when a child hurts himself and cries, for an adult to say, 'Stop crying it's not hurting', even though this may have been said to us when we were children. The child knows it's hurting. To prove his point he'll probably cry even louder. It's much smarter to listen to the child and accept his view— after all, he's the one who is hurting. It's better to say, 'I'll bet that hurt', and give an appropriate amount of comfort such as an inspection of the area, a hug and perhaps an adhesive strip. Then he won't need to scream louder to prove his point. His feelings have been respected and he is likely to get back to play much sooner.

RESUSCITATION

You can save a life if you know what to do in an emergency. The best thing to do is to sign up for a St John Ambulance or Red Cross first-aid course so that you'll be ready trained if an emergency occurs. In the meantime, read this section. Resuscitating is about A, B and C. First A, then B, then C.

A is for airway
- Clear any visible material (that is, gunk such as vomit) from the mouth and nostrils. As well as helping clear the airway, this also means that if you have to do mouth-to-mouth resuscitation (see B) you won't blow any of this gunk further into the airway, making things worse, and you won't get it all over your own mouth.
- Tilt the head back a little so that the chin is lifted. This will bring the child's tongue away from the back of the throat. Don't do this if there is a possible injury to the neck as this

type of movement may damage the spine. Spinal damage can occur in diving accidents when swimming or in head injuries. There is no need to tilt the head in infants.

B is for breathing

- Is the child breathing? Look, listen and feel for breathing.
- If not, pinch the child's nostrils closed and breathe firmly into his mouth. The child's chest should rise when you do this. In infants, because the nose and mouth are so close, just cover the nose and mouth with your own mouth and blow. Give two or three good breaths like this.
- If breathing doesn't commence, start chest compression (see C) while you keep up the breathing.
- If there is no response after one minute, call an ambulance (dial 000) and continue chest compression and breathing until help arrives.

C is for circulation

- If there is no spontaneous breathing, start chest compression at the rate of 100 compressions per minute with two breaths after 30 compressions. The combination of giving breaths and compression of the chest is CPR (cardio-pulmonary resuscitation).

Until fairly recently, it was taught to feel for a pulse and to start chest compression if no pulse could be felt. The problem with that advice is that it's not all that easy to feel the pulse and often precious time, time which should have been used doing CPR, is lost. Sometimes this delay made the difference between life and death.

The basis of CPR (cardio-pulmonary resuscitation) is 'Push Hard–Push Fast'.

'Push Hard' means that you have to push on the lower half of the breastbone hard enough to compress the chest by one-third. If you are resuscitating a child, you may be able to push hard enough to do this with one hand, or with just two fingers of one hand for an infant. If you are resuscitating an adult, you'll probably need to use two hands. Place the heel of your hand over the lower half of the breastbone and put the heel of your other hand on top of that one and push down firmly keeping your elbows straight. What you are doing when you compress the chest is squeezing the heart and forcing blood through it. That's why you have to push hard enough, to make sure that the chest is compressed adequately. If you are not moving the chest sufficiently, you're not squeezing the heart.

'Push Fast' means that you need to do 100 compressions of the chest every minute. Yes, that's right, more than one every second. It's hard work, but it can be life saving. After every 30 chest compressions, give two breaths and then quickly go back to your job of chest compression.

The concept of 'Push Hard' (that's right, hard enough to compress the chest by one-third) and 'Push Fast' (yes, you've now remembered that it's 100 compressions per minute with two breaths after every 30 compressions) and not wasting time feeling for a pulse, applies to all age groups, infants right through to adults, so it's easy to remember.

If there is no response after one minute, call an ambulance (preferably call out for someone else to make the call while you keep up the chest compressions and breathing) and continue CPR until help arrives. I've seen quite a number of children whose lives were saved, particularly after a near-drowning, by someone giving prompt CPR. So it does work.

It is clearly unrealistic to do CPR with an instruction book beside you, particularly if you have to search the house for the book, finally remembering that you lent it to somebody. So this section is really to remind you of the basics of CPR and to encourage you to sign up for a course to learn to do it properly.

Although the basics of CPR remain the same, new research often leads to small variations in the technique, so what you have read previously may not necessarily be up to date in a couple of years and what you read now may be a little different a year or two later. However, the basic technique, involving A, B and C, will remain the same.

Anyhow, you're probably more likely to need to use CPR on your partner than on your grandchild, another reason for becoming proficient in its use.

Appendix:
Some Useful Resources

If you check out all the information on the following websites, you'll be a real know-all. You might just drive your children crazy with your authoritative advice. While it's interesting stuff, perhaps it's better not to be your main source of conversation with your children. After all, even though we'd sometimes love to, we don't want to be in the business of telling our children how to bring up their children.

The following websites are reputable and can be relied upon for sound information.

Counselling and support services

The Association of Childrens Welfare Agencies
A peak body that was founded with the objectives of supporting non-government agencies and improving the quality of services to children and young people who need to live away from their families.

www.acwa.asn.au
Telephone (02) 9281 8822

Aunties & Uncles
This volunteer program helps to provide an extended family that children can learn to rely on and trust. The network can help with providing respite care for children at weekends and also provide support for their carers.

www.auntiesanduncles.com.au
Telephone (02) 9638 2480

Child abuse prevention

NAPCAN, the National Association for Prevention of Child Abuse and Neglect, has many written resources with emphasis on prevention of abuse and supporting families. Go to their website for phone numbers in each state.

www.napcan.org.au

Child and Family Welfare Association of Australia

This is the national peak body for child, adolescent and family welfare in Australia. Although it is New South Wales-based, its membership includes the peak child and family welfare bodies in each state.

www.cafwaa.org.au
Telephone (02) 9281 8822

Domestic violence helplines

Telephone numbers for each state:
New South Wales 1800 656 463
Northern Territory 1800 019 116
Queensland 1800 551 800
South Australia 1800 800 098
Tasmania 1800 608 122
Victoria 1800 800 098
Western Australia 1800 007 339

Family Relationships Centres

These centres have been set up to be the first port of call when families want information about relationship issues. They can help with mediation and dispute settlement within families. They provide three free counselling services and can offer telephone information, advice and referral.

Telephone 1800 050 321

Good Beginnings

This organisation provides a variety of resources including a volunteer and professional home visiting service that supports parents of young children. Good Beginnings aims to create a caring environment with families, communities, service agencies and governments working together.

www.goodbeginnings.net.au
Telephone (02) 9211 6767

Grandparents Raising Grandchildren

This organisation can provide information about support services, legal and financial information as well as about respite care and regular news updates.

www.raisinggrandchildren.com.au

Telephone (02) 9286 3860

Grandparent support groups

The groups provide information on support services for Australians aged over 50 who have taken on the role of parenting. Grandparent support groups are in each state.

www.seniors.gov.au

When you get to that website, go to the 'search' section and type in 'grandparents as parents'. This will take you to some useful resources and will list the grandparenting support groups throughout Australia.

Grandparents Australia (the national support group):

Telephone (03) 9372 2422

The Mirabel Foundation

Established to assist children who have been orphaned or abandoned due to parental drug use and who are now in the care of extended family. The foundation produces a useful information book *When the Children Arrive...*

www.mirabelfoundation.com

Telephone (03) 9527 9422

Families and family assistance

Anglicare Australia

A national network of care and social justice agencies of the Anglican Church in Australia.

www.anglicare.asn.au

Telephone 132 622

Barnardos Australia

A non-denominational, non-government child welfare agency.

www.barnardos.org.au

Telephone 1800 061 000

Centacare

Catholic Social Services Australia, the peak national body for social services of the Catholic Church.

www.centacare.com.au
Telephone (02) 6285 1366

Childcare (National Childcare Accreditation Council)

The National Childcare Accreditation Council has a register of family day schemes and long day centres across Australia. You will be able to find details of facilities and their accreditation status in your area on their website.

www.ncac.gov.au and then click on the link 'Search for Child Care'

Commonwealth Carers Respite Centres

May be able to help for emergencies where you suddenly become unable to provide care, such as a short stay in hospital. They can give advice about respite services and phone service closest to you.

Telephone 1800 059 059, or you can find more information on the website www.health.gov.au but it's probably quicker to type 'Commonwealth Carers Respite Centres' into Google, at least I found it was much quicker.

Family Law Hotline

General information about family law may be obtained by calling the Family Law Hotline. This is a free telephone information service for people experiencing family and relationship problems.

Telephone 1800 050 321

Law Council of Australia

You can also try the Family Law website set up by the Law Council of Australia (www.lawcouncil.asn.au) or the Australian Law Online website (for this one, it's easier to just type 'Australian Law Online' into Google).

St Vincent de Paul Society

An arm of the Catholic Church, which provides a variety of support services.

www.vinnies.org.au
National Council Office: telephone (02) 9572 6044

The Salvation Army
The Salvos provide a wide range of welfare and support services, and a care line.
www.salvos.org.au
Telephone 1300 363 622

Single parents
Support and guidance for single parents is available from Parents Without Partners.
www.pwp.org.au
General parenting guides are available from Parentlink.
www.parentlink.act.gov.au/parenting_guides

The Smith Family
An independent charity supporting disadvantaged Australian children.
www.thesmithfamily.com.au
Telephone (02) 9085 7222

General information

Australian Institute of Family Studies
A resource with a variety of information and research on families and children, from infant temperament through to child abuse, and plenty in between.
www.aifs.gov.au
Telephone (03) 9214 7888

Choice
'Choice' is the voice of the Australian Consumers Association. Choice publishes a book that is regularly updated called *The Choice Guide to Baby Products* which gives information about what safety features to look for when purchasing items for babies.
www.choice.com.au
Telephone (02) 9577 3333

Raising Children Network

An excellent website with lots of useful information about children of all ages, it even has a grandparents section. It also includes information on children with disabilities, dealing with separation, step-parents, single parents, same-sex parents, raising children from different cultures, mental illness, adoptive parents, teenage parents, parents with physical disability and parents who are drug users, with links to other useful sites.

www.raisingchildren.net.au

Television and the media

Young Media Australia is committed to the promotion of the healthy development of Australian children. It provides helpful information about the effects of media on children and strategies for parents.

www.youngmedia.org.au/mediachildren

Health

Allergies

The website of the Australasian Society of Clinical Immunology and Allergy provides useful and authoritative information on asthma, allergy and immune diseases.

www.allergy.org.au

Asthma

Up to 20 per cent of Australian children have asthma, so it is worth the whole family being well informed, particularly as there is evidence that the better informed the family is, the better the asthma is managed. Asthma Foundations Australia has a good website.

www.asthmaaustralia.org.au

Immunisation (Immunise Australia)

There is lots of erroneous and frightening information out there, largely promoted by self-styled experts with little real expertise, so beware. A reputable source is the Australian government's Immunise Australia Program.

www.immunise.health.gov.au

Telephone 1800 671 811

The Children's Hospital at Westmead

The Children's Hospital at Westmead has a wide range of fact sheets on childhood illness, nutrition and parenting on its website at www.chw.edu.au

You can also telephone Kidshealth at the Children's Hospital at Westmead. Kidshealth is a resource for parents (and grandparents) and can provide help with a variety of information.

Telephone (02) 9845 3585

The Royal Children's Hospital, Melbourne

This website also has excellent information on health and other family matters, although you'll understand why loyalty made me put the Children's Hospital at Westmead first.

Go to www.rch.org.au, click on the 'parents & families' tab and then 'kid's health information for parents'.

Healthy living

Nutrition

The Australian Nutrition Foundation gives good, general nutrition advice.
    www.nutritionaustralia.org

Obesity

A major and increasing problem in our society. Good advice is available from the New South Wales Government's Healthy and Active Kids site:
    www.health.nsw.gov.au/obesity/youth

Sex education

It's best to leave this to the parents, but if you feel your sex education was inadequate this could be a useful resource for you. Family Planning Queensland has an interactive CD, *Puberty Plus*, for children of upper primary school age.
    www.fpq.com.au

Smoking

Facts about smoking, its effects and advice about quitting are available from the Australian Council on Smoking and Health.
    www.acosh.org

Safety, first aid and resuscitation

Australian Red Cross

Provides first-aid courses and other useful information.

www.redcross.org.au

The Child Restraint Information Line

This information line has been established by the Australian Transport Safety Bureau. You can telephone them for information about suitable infant and child car restraints or print off the information by going to their website. Type in 'child car restraints' in the search box for their guide to child restraints.

www.atsb.gov.au

Telephone 1800 020 616

Kidsafe

A valuable resource on home, transport and product safety and accident prevention for children is the Child Accident Prevention Foundation of Australia's website.

www.kidsafe.com.au

Poisons Information Centre

Professional advice about what to do when children and adults swallow things they aren't supposed to. They'll tell you what the danger is and what you must do.

Telephone 131 126

The Royal Life Saving Society of Australia

Provides instruction in cardio-pulmonary resuscitation.

www.royallifesaving.com.au

Telephone (02) 8217 3111

St John Ambulance Australia

Conducts courses on cardio-pulmonary resuscitation and also has health and safety web links and phone numbers for a range of health resources.

www.stjohn.org.au

Index